The Forbidden Sermons

Written By:

Mike Hillebrecht

The Forbidden Sermons
© 2014 mike hillebrecht
ALL RIGHTS RESERVED

This work is licensed under a Creative Commons Attribution-ShareAlike 3.0 Unported License.

ISBN-13 978-0615985503
ISBN-10 0615985505

Scripture quotations are from the King James Version.
Cover Design: SelfPubBookCovers.com/eLaB

Other Books by mike hillebrecht
Grace for Shame
Chesed – Beyond the Veil of Mercy
Your Life is a Freaking Mess and You Want Answers
A Kingdom Primer
Eternal Life. Yes, Forever
My Grace to You

Published by
Charis Academy Publishing
Portland, Oregon
www.charisacademy.org

Table of Contents

Chapter 1 6

Chapter 2 12

Chapter 3 21

Chapter 4 29

Chapter 5 38

Chapter 6 44

Chapter 7 49

Chapter 8 62

Chapter 9 73

Chapter 10 77

Chapter 11 90

Chapter 12 102

Chapter 13 109

Chapter 14 130

Chapter 15 138

Scripture Reference 143

Chapter 1

"Good morning. This is Leon Scheffield. How may I help you?"

"Yes, good morning. This is Tim Bussle. I pastor a church here in Clairmont. I was at a pastor's meeting over in Delany about eight months ago where you were one of the main speakers."

"Yes, I remember the conference. I can't say that I recall meeting with you Tim, but what can I do for you?"

"No, we didn't get a chance to meet during the break out sessions due to a change in my schedule which called me away unexpectedly. I was going through my notes from the meeting and I wrote down a statement you made…let's see where is it?" Tim asked flipping through the notebook sitting on his desk before him. "Hmm…my apologies, I'm generally more prepared than this…yes! Here it is. You said, *'Playing church isn't enough to give you a good night's sleep. We've all played too long and have nothing to show for it.'* So the reason for my call…"

"When are you going to close the doors?" Leon interrupted.

"Huh, what?" Tim asked with confusion.

"You heard me. When are you going to give up your ministry and close the doors?"

"I'm n-n-not closing the d-doors," Tim stammered.

"Okay, so you're grooming your replacement, probably your assistant pastor. Or, heaven forbid, you still have to get the clearance from your board to even ask him if he would like the spot. So which is it?" Leon pressed.

"I don't need a board's clearance...wait a minute! What is going on here? I called you to get some advice and you jump to the conclusion that I'm going to leave this congregation in the hands of someone who's not ready for the kind of heat he'll face from them. I guess you're not the person who has the answers I'm looking for."

"You're absolutely right Tim. I'm not the person with the answers. You are. You know it. The issues that you're facing at your church right now can't be solved by some consultant. There are defects in the foundation of how your body was assembled. It does not matter how many seminars, programs, or quick-fix messages you try to apply, the structure is only as strong as what its foundation has been designed to carry. Do you understand what I mean?" Leon asked in a fatherly manner.

"Yes, I do." Tim quietly responded.

"Good. If you still don't want me to help, that's fine. But let me ask you a few questions before you've completely made up your mind. Okay?"

"Yeah, sure I guess."

"So did you start this church or were you hired?" "I was hired about 12 years ago." Tim cautiously answered.

"Have you ever run a church before this one?" Leon asked. "No, I was an associate for 5 years in a medium-sized church before me and my family moved here."

"How many people do you have on staff, full and part-time?" "Four full time and three part-time."

"Is your wife involved in the ministry?" Leon cautiously asks. "Uh…hmm…not right now. She…we have decided that she needs a break," Tim hesitantly replies.

"Good! Breaks do a world of good. So let me ask you one last question, are you in a building program right now?" "No, our facility is paid for and suits the needs of our people."

"Alright Tim, I got the information I was looking for and it does confirm my initial assessment. You inherited a structurally flawed body which is slowly rotting away from their previous revelation. Hopefully, you noticed how I didn't ask anything about the makeup of your congregation. I really don't need to if you're like all the other churches in this country. You're losing your older population, not to death, but to their RV's and grandkids. Kids you have plenty of, from single parents to families, but you can't hold on to them once they graduate high school. You have a handful of young adults who float in and out and you can't seem to get them to commit to being a part of the community. Most of your families whose kids have graduated school are only represented by the mother during most weekly services. The men who you do have attending, if you seriously asked them why they're coming, will tell you first that it's because of their wife or kids. You probably have an altar call every service, but honestly, there hasn't been a new convert in quite a while, which means you're just going through the motions with the same people. Lastly, if there is any outside ministry that you're doing in the community, if truth be told, one of a dozen other churches are doing it also. So if you quit doing it today, it wouldn't make an impact at all in the community. Did I miss anything?" Leon asks.

"Whew...no. You were pretty much on the mark," Tim replied with resignation in his voice.

"So Tim, as I said, I'm not the one with the answers, you are," Leon stated.

"Leon, I may have been a little quick in my assessment about that," Tim apologized.

"Tim, how long have you and your wife been talking about getting out of there? What a year, maybe more? But whatever brought it all to a head, the thing which required her to need a 'break,' still keeps ticking, right?" Leon skillfully inquired.

"Okay...yes, yes, yes, yes. God help me, Leon, I don't know what to do, even though you seem to think otherwise," Tim broke down as tears from years of frustration began to stream down his cheeks.

Leon paused for a moment to allow Tim to compose himself. "Tim, about 16 years ago I was sitting in the same seat you're in right now, faced with the exact conditions both at home and in my church. I too did not know what to do. I cried out to God for hours, weeks and months for help and I never found any.

"One day an elderly man came into my office. I'd never seen him before that time either in my church or in town even though I found out latter he used to be the town butcher. I was quite surprised at his appearance. He introduced himself and gave me the firmest, warmest handshake I have ever had from that day 'til now. As we held a position of greeting he reached into his vest pocket and pulled out a card and handed it to me. 'Son, it's time to cut the fat and do what you know to do. Call this man and he'll make the first slice for you.' I didn't have time to ask what he meant because he released my hand and walked out the door. I was so mesmerized by the whole incident that I didn't even follow him.

"I picked up the phone and called the man, Carl Jenson. When he picked up the phone and I mentioned how I had gotten his number from the elderly gentleman, the first words out of his mouth were, 'When you going to close the doors?' I must say Tim, I put up a little stronger fight than you did, but it didn't matter, the result was the same."

"So what happened?" Tim anxiously asked.

"You called me. That should say enough. I'm going to tell you what Carl told me because it's what's going to happen to you if you want it. The first thing you need to discover is whether you are called to the work of the Lord. If you feel you truly are, then you're going to have to go back to the beginning and build on the one true foundation of Christ. I'll show you what this is and how you do it if you're not certain after all this time what it truly looks like. As you do this your ministry will lose the fat which is killing you. I will come and give the primary teaching your people will need to set the course for your work in the months ahead. This is the teaching you can't give. It is the forbidden sermon…"

"The forbidden sermon? What kind of sermon title is that?" Tim laughed.

"It's the most important one that you and your congregation will ever remember," Leon briskly correct him. "You can't give this because it has such a radical effect on congregations that you can't be the one to deliver it and then be expected to deal with what follows afterwards."

"You make it sound like my farewell message," Tim exclaimed.

"No, it's your welcome message. Your people will know afterwards where they, and you, stand in the whole design of how things will operate."

"What's this going to cost me?" Tim asked hesitantly.

"If you've already given yourself to the Lord, nothing. But if you haven't, let me just say you can't afford to not do this. The only question I have for you Tim is this: What date do you want me make the first cut?"

Chapter 2

"Thank you, Pastor Tim. It is a great privilege and pleasure to be here with the people of God today. If you'll please remain standing, I would like to conduct a brief poll." Taking his bible in his hand and raising it over his head, Leon addressed the crowd, "If you have a bible with you here today would you please raise it up high so I could see it."

There was a shuffling from the seats of the congregation as hands lifted bibles proudly into the air. "That's good. Probably about 200 I reckon," Leon stated as he scanned the congregants in the building. "Do you realize there are more bibles in this one meeting alone then were in the entire city of Jerusalem, and possibly even in the country of Israel, during the days of Jesus?"

Leon watched the expressions of surprise from many of the people as they turned and looked about the auditorium at the bibles which were raised up. "As a matter of fact, if you were around in the days of Jesus, simply because you can read, you would be in the upper rung of the religious class. So those of you who have raised up your bible, if you could do me a personal favor, please close it up, neatly tuck it under your seat and please be seated. For those of you who didn't have a bible please remain standing."

The rustling of papers along with hushed whispers filled the chamber as people followed the directions which had been given to them. "Good," responded Leon after several minutes. "Let's see, one...two...three..." began Leon as he pointed at the remaining people standing. "...ten...eleven... and twelve. Isn't this something! Same number as Jesus' disciples," he quipped as the body of people snickered at his reaction of joy.

"The bible claims that there is no condemnation to those who are in the Spirit. I want each of you to know how I don't have you standing here in order to point out your lack of having a bible, but to applaud you for coming here expecting to hear a fresh word directly from the Spirit. A word which will significantly impact your life for the rest of the week and change forever how you relate to God."

Sweeping his hand across the crowd, Leon responds, "I want everyone to look around and see who these valiant people of the Spirit are because after today they won't be the same when they come into your midst." Patiently he watched as the people glanced around themselves and took notice of the people standing.

"Thank you and you too may be seated," Leon stated as he walked over towards the Plexiglas lectern that presided in the middle of the platform. With slow, methodical movements he took his bible and notepad and placed them upon the lectern. Raising his eyes up to look at the congregation he stopped all motion. A hush falls over the crowd as they settle into there seats and directed their gaze toward Leon. Slowly he looked back down at the lectern and opened his bible while shifting the notepad to the side. Again, he raised his eyes towards the crowd, but this time while keeping his right hand upon the lectern he stepped to the side. The silence continued to build in the room as all eyes are focused upon Leon.

BOOM!

The sound was almost deafening while startled gasps and screams rumbled through the hall reverberating like distant thunder. Many cast furtive glances towards Pastor Tim seated on the platform, but they all quickly transfixed their gaze back on Leon erectly standing next to the fallen lectern, his bible and notebook now strewn across the platform.

"And they shall teach no more every man his neighbor, and every man his brother, saying, Know the LORD: for they shall all know me, from the least of them unto the greatest of them, says the LORD: for I will forgive their iniquity, and I will remember their sin no more," Leon spoke into the microphone with a hushed, commanding voice as he gazed piercingly out into the crowd.

"No more teaching," he said as he pointed towards the pile next to him. "NO MORE teaching," he emphasized as he pointed towards the front row of associate pastors. Bending over and picking up his bible, "NO MORE TEACHING," he boldly proclaimed as he threw his bible down the center aisle of the auditorium. Gasps rippled through the crowd as it landed with a thud and spun wildly down the carpet.

"This verse, out of the 31st chapter of Jeremiah, follows the most important declaration made in all the bible, which is found in verse 31, where it states …"

Witnessing many of the congregation reaching under their seats and pulling out their bibles, "WHO TOLD you to get your bibles?" Leon bellows. "There it is," he shrieks as he sweeps his pointed finger across the room. "That…that right there…is the evidence of years of teaching. Do you see it, Tim?" he responds as he calmly turns toward and approaches the head pastor.

"This is one of the many dilemmas we face today. An inability to hear caused by an impulse to do first," he says as he reached down and picked up a glass of water. "Are they listening now?" he whispered to Tim, moving the microphone behind his back and bringing the glass to his lips.

Looking out over the shocked congregation, Tim whispers, "They appear to be all yours, Leon. Give it to them."

Spinning around, Leon is confronted with a mixed bag of expressions upon the faces of the congregants. However, he quickly scans the crowd to see how the 12 people who stood without a bible are responding. He sees how down to the last one, they are all smiling and appear to be leaning in towards him anticipating what he will say next. Casually, he begins to descend the steps of the platform.

"How many unbelievers do I have in this group here today? Raise your hand, even if you don't know what this means." Patiently Leon scanned the crowd for raised hands as he maneuvered himself to the front of the center aisle. "What? Are there no unbelievers here?" he said shaking his head in mock unbelief as he viewed a crowd with no raised hands. "How many of you here are afraid at this moment to raise your hand?" he comments jokingly.

About six rows ahead of him a small boy raises his hand which is quickly shoved back down into his lap by his mother sitting next to him. "No, no. Come here son," Leon compassionately responds as he waves for the child to come forward. "It's okay, I won't bite."

Tentatively, the boy gets out of his seat and begins to walk towards the aisle only to stop and look towards his mother. With a nod of affirmation from her, he spins and makes his way around large legs and over bigger feet which have been pressed under their chair to accommodate his rite of passage to the aisle. "That's right, let him come down," Leon says as the child makes it through the row towards the aisle.

"When the disciples tried to keep the children away from Jesus, he told them to stop and let them come to him because the kingdom of God belongs to them. We must keep this in mind at all times, because while they may appear small, they are the most recent arrivals from the Father and can show us something we have lost since we arrived."

Kneeling of the floor, Leon motioned for the child to approach closer to him. "What's your name?"

"William."

"William. That's a good name. Do people call you Bill or Will or Willie?"

"Uh, yeah, sometimes, but I tell them my name is William because that is what my dad calls me." Several in the congregation snicker at his response.

"That's what your dad calls you! How old are you Will, uh William, just kidding?"

"I'm just turned seven on Monday."

"Seven. Wow! Did you have a big birthday party?"

"No, not on Monday. My dad had to work and mom wanted to wait until yesterday so I could have my friends over from school. We all went to a pizza place and I opened presents there."

"You're dad worked. What does he do?"

"He's a fireman. He's not here 'cause he's working."

"Boy! A fireman! He saves people from fire! Have you ever got to see him do that?"

"No. They don't like kids 'round that stuff. But I get to ride in the truck sometimes and make the siren and horn go off. It's real fun doing that when you come up behind a car."

"I bet it is. You must have been the one who did that to me just the other day."

"No, I haven't been in the fire truck since summer."

"Oh, okay. So tell me William how long your family been here at church?

"Got here at 9:41 'cause mom couldn't find her hair brush. She told us, 'it's 9:41 and we've missed the reading of the bulletin, again.' She hates being late." A low chuckle went throughout the assembly.

"Oh! No, I mean when did you first start coming here?" Leon responded trying to hold back the laughter building inside of him.

"Mom!" William yelled as he turned towards her. "When did we first come here?" waving one hand in the air and placing the other next to his mouth to create a megaphone effect.

"Five," she called back to him trying to hide her reddening face as everyone chuckled. "Five years ago."

"OK. Mom says five years ago," William eagerly answered as he spun back around to face Leon.

The pressure was now too great and Leon began to chuckle. "You still scared William?"

"No!"

"Good. You got any brothers or sisters?" Leon asked as he shifted his weight to keep his balance.

"My brother Ben is ten. That's him sitting next to mom," William said pointing over at his brother who was sticking his tongue out at him. William responded in like fashion.

"Can I ask you a few more questions William," Leon chuckled. "Okay."

"So you love your family, William?"

"Yep."

"Love your mom?" "Uh huh."

"Love your brother?" "Yeah, sometimes."

"Love your dad?" "Sure do!"

"Does your dad love you?" "Yup," he responded while fidgeting with his shirt tail.

"How do you know your dad loves you?" "He tells me," William answered pulling a piece of string from the edge of his shirt.

"When does he tell you that he loves you?

"When he talks to me he tells me he loves me."

"Does he always tell you he loves you?" "Uh huh."

"How often or when does he tell you this?"

"Every day when we talk. In the morning before school sometimes, or uh…at night when he turns off my light at bed."

"Wow. Is there ever a time when he doesn't talk to you?" "Nope."

"Really? Never once? What about when he's working?"

"Nah. He always calls us when he works and talks to us before I go to bed."

"Wow! That is a really special father you have William."
"Yeah."

"I'm almost finished here. William, do you love Jesus?" "Yes." "Do you love him like the members of your family?" "Yah." "Does Jesus love you?" " Yup."

"William, tell me how you know Jesus loves you," Leon asked moving the microphone close to William. "Miss Pat," he responded by pointing a figure to an older woman in the front row, "told me the bible says he does."

As chuckles filled the room, Leon asked, "Who is Miss Pat?" "She's my school teacher," he chipperly replied.

"Good, William. Thank you for sharing with us. You can go back to your seat now," Leon said as he patted William on the shoulder and directed him up the aisle.

Chapter 3

Rising to his feet, Leon looked out across the congregation. "Who is the oldest person here today? If you're…" But before he could finish his sentence a flurry of pointing fingers spread across the auditorium towards a section of seats on the side. There surrounded by a cadre of eager finger-pointing participants, sat an elderly gentleman with a wry smile leaning on a cane.

"It appears, sir, that everyone has declared you to be the oldest person in this building. How old are you?" Leon said as he approached the man.

"I'm 92."

"Excuse me, could you repeat that for the audience please," Leon said as he leaned forward and maneuvered the microphone closer towards the gentleman.

"I said I'm 92," responded a clear, authoritative voice.

"Amazing! Is there anybody here older than 92?" Leon said as swept his eyes across the crowd seeking a hand. "No one? Well sir, it is an honor to meet you. What may I ask is your name?"

"William Archibald Jensen, the third."

"What? Did you say, William?" Leon responded in a surprised manner.

"Yes, William. Most people call me Bill," he said as he took his cane and waved it towards the congregation.

"Mr. Jensen, may I also call you Bill?"

"Sure. I haven't been called William since I left home for the army. You can drop the Mr. Jenson title too. That still reminds me of my dad," Bill said as he relaxed back into the seat, allowing his cane to balance between his foot and knee.

"Okay, sure Bill. Were you and your dad close?"

"Well, yeah I guess as close as any father and son could be in those days. Trying to support a family of six kids and run a business during a depression can put a lot of demands on you," he said as he gazed off into the distance. "You didn't ask, like they do today, if you love me. You just knew it or not. Life goes on. We probably grew closer before he passed away. But that was eight years ago."

"What? Your father passed away eight years ago," Leon exclaimed. "When you were, what, 84?"

"Yeah. 84. That was a pretty bad year," he said as he pulled a handkerchief from within his inside jacket pocket and casually wiped his eyes. "Lost my dad, Becky, my wife, and Sarah, my youngest daughter all within about six months." Carefully he folded the handkerchief and placed it back into his jacket pocket.

"I'm sorry to hear that. It must have been a pretty hard time for you," Leon responded as he stretched out his hand and placed it upon Bill's knee.

"Yeah, but Pastor Tim and the people in this church helped me get past it."

"That is great to hear, Bill. How long have you been saved?"

"June 5, 1944," he boldly claimed.

"Wow! That is remarkable!" Pausing for a moment, Leon looked around the room. "Why does that date sound so familiar?" he said hoping for someone to answer him.

"You're probably thinking about the day which followed, June 6th, D-Day," Bill said as he extends his hand onto Leon's shoulder and pulled him closer. "No one in his right mind goes into that kind of hell without knowing he's settled things with God first," he almost whispers to Leon staring intently into his eyes. "Know what I mean?"

"Yes, I do, sir. It was the Mekong Delta for me," Leon claims as he stretched out his arm and crosses it over Bill's, resting his hand on Bill's shoulder. "God brought us through it then just as He does today."

"Amen," Bill happily exclaims pulling Leon towards him, enthusiastically hugging and patting him on the back. "Amen Brother." Leon responded in similar fashion as deep seated emotions flow through him.

Slowly Leon pulled himself away from Bill's embrace and raised to his feet. Pulling his handkerchief from out of his pocket, he wiped the tears from his eyes and cheeks as he viewed the multitude of tear-stained faces staring intently at him.

"Bill, it is obvious to me that you love Jesus. Have you been coming here long?" Leon asks as a small number of people begin to chuckle. "What? Is it something I said?" Leon responds with a puzzled look.

"No," answers Bill, "it's just that my family, along with two others, we were the founding members of this church about…let's see, how long has it been? John was three when we moved into the Peoria Street house… so that woulda been…um…58 years ago. My goodness! Sure sounds like a long time when you say out loud like that."

"58 years!" Leon exclaims as a several people begin to lightly applaud. "Yes, by all means, Bill truly deserves a great round of applause," Leon exhorts everyone. The sound of applause begins to swell as one by one people stand to their feet and begin to cheer until everyone is joyously celebrating the works of Bill's life within their community. Occasionally Bill waves his cane in the air as recognition of their support but mostly he just sits keeping his head lowered. As the cheering and applause subside, Bill leans forward and removes a handkerchief from his back pocket and wipes his eyes and brushes it gently across his nose.

"Well Bill, it is very obvious that the people here today honor you very much. So as a founding member…wow, that is remarkable…so you've probably been involved a lot with what's been going on here. Can you tell me a little bit about that?" Leon asks as he kneels down. "What have you done here?" he says directing the microphone towards Bill.

"You're right I've been involved with a lot here. Mostly teaching has been my duty here, kids, young adults, new believers, bible studies and a number of different subjects. I've helped in the kitchen, been the janitor, parking attendant, worked with the prison ministry; I've been the shuttle driver for the kids in the bible school, an usher and a greeter. I've done pretty much anything that needed someone to fill in," Bill said in matter-of-fact tone.

"Amazing! No wonder everyone knows who you are. You've practically raised all of them!" Leon chuckled.

"Yeah, I guess I have," Bill laughed.

"With all you've done, here what is the one thing you're most proud about?"

"I've done all those things because I love the Lord and I want people to know him. There isn't one thing that I could single out that I would be proud of because pride is of the enemy," Bill said sternly.

"That is correct, Bill, pride is of the enemy. Maybe I didn't word it properly. Let me retry this. With all that you've done here for these people, with the teaching gift God placed within you, what is the most inspiring moment you've had that you keep retelling to people?"

For the longest moment Bill sat there looking off into the distance and gently tapping his cane on the floor. "Well," he finally said, "I guess it had to be the time when I led a young man to the Lord when I was working at the lumber yard just after the war. He had come in to buy a load for a house he was building for a relative of his. I found him in the yard pulling lumber from the stacks. I went up to ask him if there was something he needed that I could help him with, when he pulled a board and the stack fell over on him pinning his legs to the ground.

""He was screaming in pain trying to get out from under the load. I rushed to his side and quickly began to throw the lumber off of him. As I picked up the last board, we got the first look at how his foot was turned backwards. That was a sight I've never forgotten." Bill said shaking his head.

"That's terrible! What did you do next?" Leon anxiously asked.

"Well this guy just began screaming a whole lot more at the sight of his foot. Some of the workers in the yard are running over to us by now and they're just standing there looking at this foot. No one seems to think about going to get some help. In the midst of this, I hear this voice say to me, 'Fix it.' I can't really explain it but I knew what the voice meant. So while this guy is screaming bloody murder and the guys in the yard are yapping about how ugly it looks, I take a hold of his leg and said, 'Jesus says you're fixed.' "

"For a moment, this guy continued to scream in pain. Then suddenly his foot gave a jerk and corrected itself. Then everybody screamed. I looked at the guy and his eyes are almost falling out of his head. I asked him if he can feel anything different. All he can say is, 'What just happened? What did you do?'"

"I helped him to his feet and proceeded to walk him around a bit. All the while he's asking, 'What happened? What's going on here?' After the guys in the yard finally left us, I asked him if there was anything else he needed that I could help him with. He pulled me towards him, with tears in his eyes and said, 'I know somehow, someway, a miracle happened here. You've got to tell me, why me?'"

"I then told him how Jesus died for his sins and how Jesus told me his foot was fixed. So I just followed what He told me. Then this guy looks at me and says, 'Do you do this often?' I told him it was the first time I had ever had anything like that happen. Then he asks me if there is any way he might be able to do the same thing. I told him he needed to be saved first and then maybe Jesus would work through him too. I then led him in a sinner's prayer and prayed for him. I never saw him again."

"That is truly an amazing testimony, Bill. Had you started this church when that happened?"

"Oh, no, this church didn't start until a few of years after that," Bill answered.

"I see. Again, that is remarkable. Praise God! Don't you think so everyone?" Leon asks as he turns toward the congregation. Many responded with clapping and cheers. Leon mades his way back toward the center aisle surveying the approving response of the crowd. As they settled into their seats Leon looked at his bible which still lay in the aisle 15 feet in front of him. Slowly he strode up the aisle where it lay and bent over to pick it up, gently unfolding the pages which had been bent in its flight and landing.

"Pastor Tim, asked me to come here today and speak to you about a subject which is very vital to the life of your congregation," Leon began as he turned toward the front of the sanctuary and began to slowly walk down the aisle. "I told him I could only tell you what you already know to be true. It would be from this truth where you would either accept or reject what I say. Either way, the life or death of this congregation would rest on truth. So how many of you are willing to hear the truth leading to life?" Leon asked, reaching the front of the sanctuary and turning towards the people. A flurry of hands raised in the air accompanied with numerous "Amen," just as Leon expected.

"Good. Let me ask you a question to start this off. If I were to create a scale represented by young William," he said pointing to the young man on his left, "on one end, and by Bill," he said pointing to the elder on his right, "on the other end, where would you fall for how much God loves you?"

Chapter 4

It was the perfect setup. Leon skillfully paused and watched as the congregants deeply thought about the question. Throughout the audience he could see the few who were perplexed by the standard given to rate the love of the Father. However, those were overwhelmed in the responses provided by glances toward the two participants who had been chosen to model the spectrum of the field.

"If this were a truly a scientific endeavor, I would ask by a showing of hands who saw themselves more aligned with young William or with Bill. However, in order to avoid any controversy in such a display, allow me a moment to clarify what each of these people represents for those who might not fully understand what is being asked here.

"Young William represents a child in Christ. They don't know the fullness of what they have entered into and just live each day as it comes. They don't have any expectations and just do what they are told. They know that they love the Father and He in turn loves them.

"Bill, on the other hand, represents maturity. There have been battles, won and lost, but perseverance to stay the course has prevailed. There is an obligation to complete the "things of God" in every endeavor. The fear of God is a prime emotion in all the work that is done.

"So with this being said, using these two people as depictions of a scale, where would you fall for how much God loves you?"

Leon could see from the expressions of the people how this refinement of the scale had solidified many of their decisions. Those who seemed somewhat perplexed at the beginning now were aligning themselves with one of the candidates. "By a show of hands, how many of you have an answer to this question," Leon asked as he scanned the room. Rapidly, an overwhelming majority of the congregation thrust their hands into the air.

"There is an old Jewish saying," Leon began, "that goes like this, 'When faced with two choices, always pick the third one.' I say this because if you were to answer my question, no matter how you answered it, you would be wrong," he said witnessing surprise in many of the faces. "Yes, wrong. This is one of the other problems you now have to deal with. You do remember the first problem I found out here, don't you?" he asked as he lifted his bible towards them and scanned the crowd.

"For those of you who want to hear it correctly, here are the two first problems I've detected: 1. A reliance on the written word of God which supersedes the spoken word of God; 2. A scale of worthiness that you believe God measure yours efforts by in order to receive his love. The scriptures are very clear how God is no respecter of person." As Leon said this he watched as many throughout the audience began squirming in their seats or flashed expressions of surprise followed by acceptance to the words which he spoke.

"There are probably many more issues which need to be addressed, and I may do so during the message I'm here to deliver, but for now I'm going to work on these two first. Recall how I stated that there are more bibles in this room than were in all of Jerusalem, and perhaps Israel, at the time of Jesus. How many of you have prayed for God to make you and your church more like the first day church?" Leon asked as a flurry of hands sheepishly waved in the air. "How many of you have pleaded for the power of the Holy Spirit flow to through you just like it did in the book of Acts?" As a more emboldened response of hands in the air came, he asked, "How many of you have pressed so hard into God to live a life like the book of Acts that you have carpet burns on your forehead, knees and elbows?"

As chuckles swarmed around the room and few people quickly raised and lowered their hands, Leon raised his bible above his head. "This," he said waving his bible furiously, "is the one thing that they didn't have in their day and they accomplished more than we do with it. How can this be?

"The prophetic words of God resonated throughout the land of Israel in the days of Jesus to such a degree that people were anxiously waiting for the next occurrence to be confirmed. Isaiah, David, Moses, even Zechariah were all confirmed. However, the words of Jeremiah were perplexing, almost unthinkable. Issued at a time of Israel's darkest moments, from a prison cell, Jeremiah decrees how the union of Israel and Jehovah would be abolished and that the priestly system of sacrifices and atonement would no longer exist. The most shocking word was how everyone would know the Lord from the least to the greatest!

"As unbelievable as it may have been, his words too were validated. Does anybody know when this happened? Bill, do you know?" Leon asked as he looked over at the elderly man who was gently rocking in his seat.

"Yes, at the cross of Jesus," Bill responded boldly.

"Correct, at the cross. How many years has it been, anyone?" Leon asked as he swept his arm across the room of entranced faces. From the back of the room a young woman shouts, "2,000 years ago."

"That's right!" Leon exclaims as he point to the woman. "Everyone say '2,000 years ago.'"

"2,000 years ago!" they replied

"And when was the first church of the book of Acts?" Leon watches the faces of the congregation as they try to determine if they are to respond together or if someone is to answer. "2,000 years ago," come a few bold answers. "Are there only a few of you who know when the first church was?" Leon chides the group as he points to several of those who answered. Noting the heads which were nodding in disagreement to his accusation he asks, "So when was the first church of the book of Acts?"

"2,000 years ago!" came a loud, unified voice.

"Can I say that, 2,000 years ago, the first church did not have a bible and they had greater results than we do today?" "Yes," came a loud response from the crowd. "If the first church didn't have a bible, may I submit that, according to the words of

Jeremiah, they knew the Lord from the least to the greatest in a fashion we do not understand?" While numerous people shook their heads in agreement, Leon continued. "What was the mission of Jesus on the earth? Anyone?"

"To save the lost," came a voice from the side. "That's good, but this actually happened on the cross." Leon responded. "I'm talking about what was his purpose while walking on the earth."

"To heal the sick and blind," came a shout from the back of the room. "Yes, he did that, however I submit that this was a result of his purpose. Anyone else?"

"To destroy the works of the devil," came a quiet response from the front of the room. "Yes! 1 John 3:8 tells us the purpose of Jesus being manifested was to destroy the works of the devil. This same verse states how the devil sinned from the beginning. Am I safe to say that the term "beginning" in this passage is longer than 2,000 years ago?" "Yes," came several voices from around the sanctuary.

"Let me offer to you today that the manner in which Jesus destroyed the works of the devil was in revealing the Father to people. Consider that the fall of man in the garden came when they partook of the fruit from the tree of knowledge good and evil. The enemy had told them when they eat of the tree how they would be like God knowing good from evil. The purpose of all food is to sustain the body but that single bite severed their spiritual connection with the Father and produced the knowledge of doing something bad, and its ultimate reward, death. Think about how the first sin was actually trying to do something good by trying to be like God.

"Mankind has been since then striving to be good, or even just good enough, in all its endeavors so they would be accepted by the Father. You know what I mean? You're measuring yourself to some standard of approval. Striving to be accepted but never quite feeling that you're there. You look at going to more school, get a part-time job, move into a different area of town or the state; change jobs, schools, churches, doctors, banks, friends, husbands, wives; you change clothes, hairstyles, deodorants, toothpaste, cars, restaurants, diets, and nothing curbs the gnawing feeling of being unworthy.

"So you read more of your bible, pray louder and longer, buy more worship music, witness to people more, attend more meetings and bible studies, read more books, get more teaching to learn 5 ways to pray more effectively, 7 steps to rid your household of demonic influences, 4 keys to loving your spouse, 9 steps to being more fruitful and prosperous, 6 steps to raising more biblical children; 3 essential keys to turn more away from the things of "the world" to make you more holy; the list goes on. And for what? At the end of it, you're still feeling how you don't measure up.

"The truth be told, you will never measure up living from the tree of the knowledge of good and evil. Ever! You see we are only looking at half of the tree. We know how we're not evil people like… insert any bad person's name you want here. But the whole tree is good, and evil. The entire fruit production from this tree is one thing: death. The fruit is produced on the good side as well as the bad side. Sure the fruit looks attractive, sure it will make you wise, and it certainly will sustain the body. However, no matter how high you climb the tree to measure up, the fruit always produces the same result – it buries you in the ground"

Leon watched some of the expressions of the people change from surprise to disbelief, while others nodded in agreement. Pausing for a moment to allow the full impact of his words to do what was intended; he ascended the stairs, found his glass of water and took a long, slow drink.

"Let me see how many of you believe what I just described was the intention of the Father when He created the world." Slowly Leon looks out across the sanctuary for any who agreed with him while he descends the stair. Seeing no hands raise or heads nod in agreement, he paused for a moment longer. "If, by your response, no one believes this was the intent of the Father, then how come you believe that this is what you need to do to fulfill His will in your life?"

Deafening silence filled the room as Leon looked at the bewildered faces of the people. "You've possibly never thought of this, right?" he asked to the few heads agreeing in response. "Look, I've been there too. I tried to please God by my own efforts, whether it's prayer, fasting, reading my bible, you name it. Sure, in the beginning there was a rush of excitement, a thrill in knowing I was doing what it took to move the hand of God, or become more holy so I could be in His presence. But the thrill soon, often very soon, wore off and I trudged on because I had been taught this was what was required of me. This is what others had done; this was what the saints of old did, so if I was going to be anywhere near them, by God, I was going to go through it also.

"However, every time I "jumped in for Jesus," I felt like I was drowning. I knew firsthand what Peter felt like when he got out of the boat. And yes, I also remember how Jesus chastised him for having little faith. This in turn spurred me on more, faster, harder, and deeper until I just got burned out on God." Leon paused again to let the words make their fullest impact.

"How many of you have gotten burned out on God," he asked holding his hand up in the air. A small number of people across the room sheepishly extended their hand into the air. "Oh, so I see that you allow the spirit of lying to keep you in check here." He jokingly admonished those who didn't raise their hand. "Let me rephrase this then. How many of you have gotten burned out trying to be god?" A swell of chuckles rolled across the sanctuary as more people raised their hands. "How many of you are feeling like you're drowning in all the requirements you have to do to be a 'Christian?'" Now a flurry of hands raised all across the room.

"Let me tell you it is the Father's will that none of you should perish. But we must remember how His ways are not our ways and His thoughts are higher than our thoughts. The book of Hebrews tells us He seeks for us to enter into His rest. But doing all these works is not rest, right?" Leon asks rhetorically. "Yes, it also says in Hebrews we need to labor to enter His rest. However, our works, customs, rules of order, whatever you want to call it, are not the meaning of the word 'labor.'

"You see, those things which I've mentioned are "our ways, our thoughts." They are spawned from the tree of the knowledge of good and evil. As someone who is reborn we have become a new creation, the old things have passed away. One of those things is the nature of good and evil working within us. This is what Romans 7 is dealing about. But that is for a much later discussion. The dilemma we encounter is how we came into the kingdom."

Chapter 5

"How many of you here are saved?" Leon asked. As he looked out across a room full of hands extended into the air, he continued his inquiry. "That looks like most of you. Let me ask you something about your salvation experience. How many of you got saved because you didn't want to go to hell?" Again, the same hands extended into the air. "Good. How many of you got saved because when you die, you want to spend eternity with God in heaven?" Once again hands waved proudly in the air.

"I know you're arms are probably getting tired from all of this exercise, so I'm only going to ask one more question. How many of you have read the second to the last chapter of the book of Revelations where it states how eternity will have us staying on earth with God?" Leon patiently looked at the group as no one lifted their hand in response to his question. After purposely waiting several minutes, he finally broke the deafening silence. "With all of the teaching the church receives every week of every year, this is the one truth that seems to be intentionally overlooked. Because of this, death, not Jesus, has become its savior."

There was a sudden jerk of bodies that rippled throughout the congregation. This was just the response Leon expected. "You heard me correctly. Jesus is not your savior; death is, if your only purpose of salvation was to go to heaven for eternity. Many of you probably accepted Jesus with a question which went something like, 'If you were die tonight, do you know where you'd spend the rest of eternity?'" Leon watched as a majority of their heads shook in agreement.

"Consider how the gospel you agreed to was based on scaring you into God's kingdom. 1 John tells us God is love and that perfect love casts out fear. So why would God employ fear to get you saved?"

Leon watched the startled expressions on their faces. "You people look like a bull frog in a hail storm. Hasn't anyone here ever thought this out? Of course not! You're all faithful sheep who listen and follow what is being said to you. Why? Simply because you still operate for the tree of the knowledge of good and evil. Or a better term would be you function from a 'sin consciousness.'

"You were told you were a sinner and God wouldn't have anything to do with you in that state. Then you're scared into thinking how for all eternity you'll never be with God but stuck in the fires of hell, where torment will be your constant companion. So you decide to accept Jesus as your savior and spare yourself from hell. However, it's not too long before you discover how you're still tainted somehow and need to a.) Read your bible regularly; b.) Set aside a designated time to pray, which will include confessing the sins which you've done from the day; and c.) Asking for God's forgiveness once more. Now when you go to church, you become more aware how there is even further sin in your life as the pastor tells you of the need to come forward and recommit your life to God who will forgive you your sins.

"Day in and day out this is your 'new life,' finding sin, confessing sin, repenting of sin, seeking forgiveness of sin. It never ends. You become proficient in spotting it, not only in your life but in the life of family and friends, even people you don't know. You are consumed with ridding it from your life, community, and nation. Everywhere you turn it shows up.

"Now you're meeting with people who are dealing with the same issue. All of you are disgusted with its prevalence in the schools, on the television, in the music, and on the big screen. You and your group boycott businesses because they promote sin in the people they hire, or because one of the products they make, among their fifty others you regularly use, leads people to commit sin. You all gather together and fervently pray for God to hear you and remove this plague from the midst of your life, but in the back of each one of your minds you don't think He can hear you because it's all this sin which is keeping Him from you.

"You don't have to raise your hands because I know this is where you are, or have been," Leon responds. "This is the result of sin consciousness. A mind transfixed on sin. You're taught about it; you develop it, and perform it. It's a viscous cycle, a treadmill of the enemy designed to wear you down. It's a product from the tree of the knowledge of good and evil.

"It even influences how you read your bible. Scriptures which are liberating become shackles to a sin nature which won't give up the rules which bind it. Case in point: I'm a sinner saved by grace. Show of hands, how many of you know this isn't a verse in the bible?" Leon taunted the crowd. While the members of the congregation looked at each other in bewilderment, Leon pressed them further. "So how many of you have said this?" The vast majority of the people in the room raised their hands. "Okay, keep your hands up. How many of your whenever you've said this identified yourself as a sinner rather than a child of God?" Leon carefully scanned the crowd to see the hands which would lower but there was not one which came down.

"I see. You can put your hands down," Leon responded. "Let me take another tack with this. Yes, with a rising of your hands again, how many of you sinned this past week?" Hands rose throughout the building. "Okay, now I'm about to say something which is going to cause your head to explode. However, just so you know that it's not my words I'm saying, reach under your seats and get your bible out." Leon waited as everyone who had bibles quickly grabbed their bible and placed it in their laps.

"Listen carefully. For all of you who raised your hand indicating that you sinned this week, according to 1 John 3:8 you are of the devil and Jesus came to destroy your works." Leon watched throughout the congregation as eyes widened, or cheeks grew red in anger. "It's not me saying this, go see for yourself. 1 John 3:8." Leon paused and watched people throughout the building quickly grab their bible, and frantically open it turning pages trying to locate the passage he had given them. Slowly, one by one, heads began to shake in disbelief as they raised their eyes toward Leon.

"This is the depth and breadth of living from the tree of good and evil. Here is where most religious services would stop. They've managed to make you feel like maggots in the mud of life's misery. Isn't this how you feel," he asks gently. Many people shake their heads in agreement. "The next thing they would ask you to do is come to the altar and confess your sin to God and repent from your devious ways. Isn't that right, Tim?" He says turning towards the Pastor on the stage. Startled at his name being called, Tim hesitates and then nods yes to the question.

Turning back to the crowd, Leon continues. "You will feel good with all you've done for about 18 hours. Then life hits you in the face and sometime between starting your coffee and arriving at the office you've committed at least two sins and the drudgery of the sin treadmill starts all over again. Tell me, honestly, since you've all said you're saved, where is the, quote, good news, unquote, in all of these works you're doing to be good?"

Leon looked intently at the sullen expressions of the people who understood the gravity of the message Leon was presenting to them. Many were now slumped back in their seats, head cocked back, staring blankly into space. As he turned and walked back to the steps to ascend the stage, he caught a glimpse of Bill sitting in his seat, staring at Leon. Quickly, he stepped over to him and moving the microphone behind his back, he responded, "You doing alright, Bill? Never heard truth like this before, huh?" Bill nodded his head in affirmation to the questions. "Don't worry; I'm not leaving them hanging." Leon assured the elder and then moved back up the stairs of the platform seeking his water.

Chapter 6

Taking a slow, lingering drink, Leon continued to watch the responses of the congregation. Methodically, he walked over to the edge of the stage, moved a few cords with his foot which were before him. Then squatting down, he seated himself on the edge allowing his legs to dangle down.

"What you just heard is the standard message which is delivered every Sunday across this nation through every denomination. It may change up a little bit but, boil it down, and this is what you'll get. I don't blame the world for not wanting to have anything to do with the church. All they keep hearing is the message of self-righteousness cloaked in sin-consciousness. The church has forgotten how to proclaim the truth of the gospel, a gospel the apostles preached which turned the world upside down. I can assure you making people feel like crap doesn't make them want to enter your doors and stay around."

A loud gasp rumbled throughout the auditorium. Young members giggled and pointed fingers at Leon while tugging on the sleeve of the adult they sat next to. "What! Has no one ever used that word around here? Come on people, get real. You've used worst just trying to get a parking space here," Leon reprimanded them.

"My dad said it today!" came a small voice from the middle of the congregation. Chuckles exploded from the people as some heads turned to see where the child was who made the comment.

"See. Kids are real. You can't hide things from them no matter how much you try. That's part of the reason Jesus said that the kingdom of God belongs to the children. Purity of heart and a desire to be near the Son and the Father. This comes from understanding the simplicity of the true gospel.

"Yes, you heard me correctly, the true gospel. This means there are multiple gospels floating around out there. If you doubt me on that, just consider the exercise we just completed. That is one type of gospel. I don't know what's so good about it, but people seem to clamor for it every week in person or on TV or radio. But the apostle Paul dealt with this same issue in the book of Galatians. He even calls the church fools because they had been seduced to follow a different gospel contrary to what he taught them. Do you think Paul would make the same statement to you if he were here today? You better believe it.

"Look I'm not here to beat you into a bloody, quivering mass of flesh. There are better men of the cloth who could do that for you and you'd gleefully pay them for the experience. Actually, Pastor Tim called me here today to deliver what is known as the forbidden message.

"As you may have noticed throughout the day I have purposely been breaking all the rules of a service in order to get and keep your attention. As a sidebar to that: If you have a roast in the oven or lunch reservations somewhere, you better leave now because I'm no where near finishing this message." A few heads turned to look at the clock which hung on the wall above Pastor Tim's shoulder. "How many here would like to hear what the forbidden message is? Oh, wait. I probably ought to tell you why it's called the forbidden message. It's called this because it is the one message every pastor, teacher, elder, choir director, youth pastor - you name the role – this is the one message they know but they can't reveal it because it would cause them to lose the one thing they so dearly try to hold on to: the control of the congregation.

"Yes, Pastor Tim is as guilty of this as I was. But this type of ministry takes its toll on everything you touch. Your family, children, wife, friends, board associates, ministry members, everyone gets touched by it. However, your pastor has recently embraced what some denominations would call "the dark side" of the gospel. So with that introduction, who is still interested in hearing what this message is?"

Across the sanctuary, hands quickly raised in response to Leon. Scanning the audience with approval, Leon glanced over his shoulder to see Tim holding his hand up in the air, sitting on the edge of his chair, bouncing his leg in anticipation. "Well alright then. Let me start off with these two points which summarize the entire message. First, you are greatly loved; second, you can't screw this up. Write this down because I assure you after you hear what I'm about to say, the simplicity of this statement needs to be memorialized on your mind."

Leon watched as several searched for something to write with or upon. After a few moments, he continued, "First, you are greatly loved; second, you can't screw this up. Everybody got it? Now I've had some people say to me how this statement can be condensed down to, 'You're greatly loved so you can't screw this up.' The trouble is we humans, by design, are creatures of pattern recognition. This is how we so easily store and categorize information in our brain.

"Let me show you. I want you to quickly recall four or five times in your life where you've screwed up." Leon watches as the people scan their brain for the relevant answers. After about a minute, he jokes, "Stop! Some of you are pulling up too many! And for those of you who couldn't come up with anything, you then need to see one of the staff members here," pointing to the people sitting in the front row, "and have them deliver you from that deceiving spirit you're harboring." Some of the parishioners chuckle with a couple of wives jabbing their husband in the side with their elbow.

"Okay, take about the same amount of time to recall those times in your life when you've experienced the Father's love. Go!" After waiting a few minutes he announced, "Stop! How many of you were able to recall four or five demonstrations of the Father's love in your life? Show of hands." Across the room only a couple of people raised their hand. How many of you could only recall one, maybe two, instances? Show of hands." A flurry of hands rose high in the air.

"This is the reason why you can't combine the two points together," he said sweeping his hand across the room. "None of you had any trouble coming up with your screw ups. However, the moment we recall the love of the Father, we get so caught up in what He's done for us that it blocks out all other things. Did any of you notice how the feeling that you had when you recalled your messes are gone also?" Many of the people acknowledged Leon shaking their heads in agreement. "What you're going to grow into over the days, weeks, months, and years as a result of hearing this message is experiencing this feeling of being loved whenever you recall a screw up. I know this doesn't seem possible now, but trust me, it will happen.

"This brings up a point which needs to be made right at the start. This message is a message of responsibility. Many people try to avoid being responsible. However, when you hear the truth of God's word, you will not be able to go back to the way things were before without reaping the consequences of your decision. Being responsible with this message means you accept the circumstances for every decision you make based on this truth. No longer will you be able to say, 'I didn't know,' or, 'No one told me that,' simply because I am going to tell you. Is this understood?" Leon asked.

"Okay, let's start this off. I'm not going to address these two points individually, since you've already demonstrated how they work. My intent is to reveal the depth of what God did for your screw up. This might seem counter intuitive but let me assure you, having a sin consciousness keeps you focused on the screw ups more than the love. What needs to be done is make you free, indeed."

Chapter 7

"Everyone here knows God is awesome!" Leon began to a chorus of "Amen!" "Hopefully you all know how when the man and women ate from the tree of the knowledge of good and evil, God wasn't surprised. Understand this simple truth: Wherever there is a law, the enemy will be there tempting you to break it. Breaking it gives him legal access to move into your life and wreak havoc. Jesus said the devil's mission is to, 'kill, steal and destroy.' Understand this too, if you don't know the law and accidentally break it, the enemy still has access to you. Therefore, it is your responsibility to know what the law addresses in your life."

"Actually, let me back up a moment. Raise your hand if you are or can be classified as a Hebrew by blood." Leon looked intently out over the crowd as they in turn looked out over each other trying to find a raised hand.

"It appears we do not have any hands who can claim their Hebrew heritage. This means that in the vernacular of the Hebrew language we are all known as *'goyim.'* Roughly translated, it means we are heathens. I realize this is not the most flattering term to be called, so let me use the term which the apostle Paul used in his writings; we are known as Gentiles. Is this clear to everyone?" Leon asked searching for some form of approval for the audience.

Noticing several heads shaking in agreement, he continued, "Now that we have the understanding of who we are as indicated in the bible, allow me to go back to the term 'law' and instill within you the one main theme which Paul repeats over and over again. We Gentiles do not have the Law; have never been a part of the Law; as a matter of fact, we are foreigners and strangers to it.

"There are two classes of people in the bible: Us Gentiles, and the Children of Israel. Three-fourths of the bible is the story of the children of Israel and their ability of trying to function under the covenant and law they had with God. 'The Law' is the term that represents the 613 commandments of Moses which the people of Israel had to follow to be in right relationship with God.

"Paul makes it very clear how Jesus was born under the Law and how he also is the end of the Law. The New Testament writers also plainly state that the purpose of the law was to make people think about their sins as they tried to offer sacrifices to eliminate their sinful nature.

"We Gentiles never had to follow the Law because we were never under the Law. Paul clearly states how we Gentiles are operating under grace. But somehow we've been taught that once we become a Christian, the Law, in a somewhat modified version, is acceptable for us to begin living our lives by. We believe this is what grace is about; however, this 'new law,' as every law does, develops a sin consciousness in us which we can't seem to get away from."

Leon stretched out his arm and looked at the time on his watch. "You know some of you probably need to use the restroom, get a drink, or just plain stretch," he said as he got up from where he was seated on the platform. "Let's take twenty minutes to do that and we'll meet back here to finish this matter up." As Pastor Tim approached him, Leon grabbed his arm and leaned into his ear. "We're going to see if the principles of Gideon still apply today." Tim was puzzled by this statement, but he led Leon down from the platform and through the crowd towards his office just off the main hall.

"Is there anything I can get you? Water, tea, coffee?" Tim said as he closed his office door behind him.

"No, no thanks. This break is just a part of the message," Leon responded as he moved around Tim's desk to look out the window. From this vantage point he could witness many people getting in their cars and leaving. There was a couple who were very animated in their departure. Leon watched as the man, whose face was the brightest shade of red he had ever seen, screamed at the woman to get in their car. She, poised, calm and collected, just kept shaking her head in disagreement. Suddenly, the man rushed towards the woman and grabbed her forearm, and began to push her towards the open door of the car. In an amazing feat of dexterity, the woman twisted her arm free, moved behind him and pushed him into the open door. Then she briskly walked back to the door of the church while the man was shouting at her. Leon stepped away from the window and hung his head down. "Oh, Lord, help them," he whispered.

"What are the principles of Gideon you spoke about as we walked down the platform?" Tim asked inquisitively.

"Tim, I'm going to be upfront with you. You have in this body you oversee a class of people who I've come to call over the years the 'hanger ons.' They suck the life out of you and your staff, day in and day out. They are needy, baby believers – some who may have been this way for thirty years - they want you to serve them just the milk of the word, they won't even consider the banquet of meat which awaits them.

"You know that when Gideon was preparing to go into war, God dictated to him a strategy which reduced his forces from a vast number to 300. The 'hanger ons' chose to leave and God was glorified in the battle that ensued.

"Have you ever done this same thing, you know take a break, in any of your meetings?"

"No, this is new one for me!" he chuckled.

"Well, it's an interesting device. You are about to see who in your congregation is hunger to see God move in their lives," Leon responded as he move towards the door. "Let the purging begin."

As they walked down the hall towards the sanctuary, Leon could sense a feeling of excitement in the congregation as many were scampering to get to their seats. As he entered the sanctuary people were milling around talking to their neighbor. In the distance Leon could see Bill seating stoically in his seat. The woman he had seen in the parking lot was surrounded by a group of woman who appeared to be praying for her. Quickly Leon step up onto the platform and grabbed the microphone.

"Ok. If we could all get our seats will get back into this message," he said as he unbuttoned his suit coat and laid it across an empty chair on the stage. Turning to look out over the congregation it was very apparent the about a quarter of the previous attendees were not present. Moving the microphone behind his back, he turned to Tim and said, "See. This is what I was talking about. Go tell your production people to not record the remaining part of this message."

As Tim left the stage, Leon moved to it edge and looked out over the people. "As you can see we have a few who decided that what is about to come wasn't as important as the plans they had previously made. It's possible they even think they would get the message and listen to it later. Unfortunately for them, I have requested that what is spoken here is not to be recorded. So if you could, please move forward and fill in the seats of those who have left."

People began moving into the vacant seats as Leon move down from the platform. As Tim came back towards stage, Leon said, "Tim, could you sit down here with the rest of us? I'm going to be down here for the remaining part of this message." Leon watched as the people got settled into their seats.

"How many of those who didn't bring their bible today are still us?" he asked as he scanned the audience. Hands rose up in response and Leon quickly tallied the numbers. "Nine, ten, eleven. We have only eleven of you now. Good. You'll want to get your notebooks out here since this is the only recording device still available to you.

"Alright. Let's get started. You're greatly loved and you can't screw this up. Living your life from a sin consciousness keeps you focused on the screw ups. Now I'm not talking about screw ups like putting too much detergent in the washing machine or using salt instead of sugar in a cookie recipe.

"The type of screw ups I'm talking about are those types of things that, according to some mystical ledger, make you unholy. These acts, you believe, keep God at arm's length from you. And despite all the evidence found in the bible which proves this to be unfounded, the enemy has so successfully infiltrated your thinking that when you read the bible, you discount the truths for a latter day when you're glorified.

"My plan here is to renew your mind with the gospel truth. The same truth the apostles preached and saw thousands become believers; a truth which took over the entire known world in its day. For these truths to be understood there are a few things that need to be looked at from an entirely different perspective than they have been in the traditional 'church' setting.

"First off, to you bible folks. Have you ever considered how for all which it contains, there are only three good chapters? The first two chapters in Genesis and the last one in Revelation. Everything in between is the record of man's screw up and how he tries to fix things. At no point, according to my study, does he succeed in fixing anything. Additionally, if you really want to have your brain twisted, God used murders to write most of the bible!"

At that remark, almost in unison, people gasped and snapped their heads up looking intently at Leon. "What? No ever told you that? Moses writes the first five books of the Old Testament. Killed an Egyptian and ran away," Leon states as the people begin to shake their heads in agreement.

"David writes almost all the worship songs and proverbs. Has an affair with a married woman who becomes pregnant; he sends her husband into the front of a battle and has the rest of the troops hold back, causing him to die." Now more people were agreeing with Leon's claims.

"Lastly, Paul writes more of the New Testament than any other apostle. He was more infamously known as Saul, a coat rack for those who stoned Stephen and became the religious zealot who persecuted the first church. Now if you consider these three men and the influence their writings have had on all of our lives, maybe then, just maybe, they knew something about screw ups we haven't learned yet. But I'll get to that in a moment.

"Okay, next. How many of you agree that Jesus came here to restore everything which was lost in the fall?" A loud chorus of 'Amen' followed Leon's question. "And as I pointed out from 1 John 3:8 his mission was to destroy the works of the devil. So what was his primary means of doing this?" A few hands raised across the sanctuary. Scanning the room, Leon pointed to gentleman towards the back. "You sir. What do you think the answer is?"

"He healed the sick," responded the man.

"That's a good answer, but not the correct one. Consider how Peter said that by his stripes we have been healed – an event which only occurred on his last day on the earth. Yes, the gospels also say he healed all those who were sick and oppressed of the devil. But not all were sick or oppressed. What we're looking for here is something which would destroy the works of the devil in the lives of everyone regardless of their physical condition. So any ideas?" Leon watched as the people diligently ponder the question trying to find an answer. After a few moments with no response, he decided to divulge it to them.

"The Father. He revealed the Father to them. They never knew, or better yet, never considered God as their Father. They worshipped a mighty, holy God. But to relate to him on a personal level, someone who was concerned about their very well being on a daily basis, this was something they had never experienced. This was the very first thing lost in the fall and Jesus came to restore a way of life which had not been experienced for some millenniums.

"Now I know this seems a bit strange, but remember we live 2,000 years from their revelation. Even by saying that, most of the church today has the same issue facing them – they don't know the Father. The more sin conscious they are, the farther they are from knowing our Father.

"When I say knowing Him, I'm not talking about the hundreds of sermons you've heard on 'God is love' or his redemptive names. These messages, unfortunately, have been steeped in sin consciousness. If we're going to know the Father we have got to first off agree with Isaiah 55:9 which proclaims how His thoughts and His ways are higher than ours. Only then can we grasp the significance of the phrase, 'God so loved the world that he gave…' Do you understand where I taking you with this?" Leon asked the crowd.

Many in the crowd shook their head in agreement or offered an 'amen' in response. "Pastor Tim, do you see what I'm saying? Cause if you don't then it's not going to benefit these people going any further." Pastor Tim vigorously shook his head in agreement and gave a Leon a thumbs up sign. "Good! Then I want everybody to now turn to Jeremiah 31. We're going to read a very short passage to get an understanding on the thoughts and ways of our Father. I'm telling you all here, when I get done with this today, you are going to want to get saved all over again.

"Bill," Leon said looking over at him in leaning forward in his seat, "would you be willing to read for us?" For a moment there didn't appear to be any response from Bill, but he slowly settled back into the seat and reached into shirt pocket and withdrew a pair of glasses. As he began to place them on his nose, Leon approached him. "We'll read verses 31 through 34 along with you Bill." Leon said as he extended the microphone towards him.

Holding his bible out in front of him, Bill adjusted its position until he could easily read the words with his glasses. "Jeremiah 31," Bill spoke and then began to cough a bit. "Sorry, just clearing my throat. Jeremiah 31:31. *Behold, the days come, saith the LORD, that I will make a new covenant with the house of Israel, and with the house of Judah: Not according to the covenant that I made with their fathers in the day that I took them by the hand to bring them out of the land of Egypt; which my covenant they brake, although I was an husband unto them, saith the LORD: But this shall be the covenant that I will make with the house of Israel; After those days, saith the LORD, I will put my law in their inward parts, and write it in their hearts; and will be their God, and they shall be my people. And they shall teach no more every man his neighbor, and every man his brother, saying, Know the LORD: for they shall all know me, from the least of them unto the greatest of them, saith the LORD: for I will forgive their iniquity, and I will remember their sin no more."*

"Thank you Bill. Okay, you may have recognized the last part of this passage is what I began this message on today. So what we have here is an Old Testament prophecy which declares the thoughts and ways of the Father. Does everyone agree?"

"Yes," came the response from around the room.

"Has this prophecy been fulfilled?" Leon asked. "Yes," came a loud response from the people.

"When was this fulfilled?" Murmurs came from around the room as the people gave varied responses. "Okay, so you're not so in agreement with this answer. For sake of argument on the particulars, can we agree that it was fulfilled 2,000 years ago?" Leon asked. Many of the people responded yes or shook their head in agreement.

"Good. This is the prophecy of the New Covenant we operate under. Now this is important to understand because a covenant is one of the primary ways the Father operates on this earth. While He is all powerful, all knowing, always present, He has restricted the involvement of His kingdom on this earth to only those who are in covenant with Him. He only enters into covenant with someone who out of their own free will elects to do so. He will not ever override the free will of someone who decides they do not wish to be in covenant with Him," Leon stressed while watching the reactions of the people.

"I'm going to say this again because, from your non-reaction, I don't think that you heard me. God, the Father of all creation, will never override the free will choice of someone who does not wish to be in covenant with Him." A few of the people responded with an 'amen' at Leon reiteration. "Okay, I'll leave that be for a moment since it hasn't registered yet.

"There are a number of covenants found throughout the bible, but we are concerned with just three of them. This passage in Jeremiah mentions two of them, the new covenant, or what many refer in the New Testament as the covenant of grace; and there is the old covenant of the children of Israel, more commonly called the Law as I've previously mentioned. However, the apostle Paul tells us that there was a covenant that predated the Law by 430 years which was made and mediated by Abraham. It was this covenant which guaranteed the Christ coming through Abraham's seed. I am going to submit to you right now that Abraham functioned under a covenant of grace just like we do. I don't have the time to show it all to you, but this is why you have Pastor Tim," Leon stated as he pointed at Tim.

"Okay, here is the point I need to make with Abraham's covenant of grace. When Abram is ninety-nine years old, El Shaddai calls him and says, '... walk before me and be perfect. I'm going to make my covenant between you and me and I'm going to multiply you exceedingly...' Let's start at 'be perfect.' Many years prior when God appeared to Abram he was declared 'righteous' because he believed God would give him an heir. Righteous is a legal term when you're dealing with kings. It simply means that you have favorable access to be in the presence of the king without an invitation being required.

"In the Hebrew language, this word 'perfect' means…wait for it…wait…okay, ready?. It means: Perfect," Leon states drily as people begin to laugh. "So at ninety-nine Abram is declared perfect. Don't you imagine he's thinking to himself, 'Yeah, right! What about the issues of bringing Lot with me, or the many times I had to pass my wife off as my sister? Oh and let's not forget Hagar and Ishmael.' Let me assure you, if God calls you perfect, He has already taken this into account, and frankly, He's not as bothered about it as you are.

"You know that up until this moment the Lord had always appeared to Abram as Jehovah. This is a new view of God's character which Abram gets to experience and it is appropriate at ninety-nine. Shaddia's original meaning is, many breasted one, or as I like to say, the one who is equipped to supply all needs. The significance here is how at his age, Abram could not supply his need, namely a son. Sure, Sarai had been barren, but Ishmael meant Abram still had the means within himself to produce, or meet the need. At ninety-nine, with no potency within his facility, the one who supplies all needs certifies a covenant with a sign displayed at the one place where the weakness is the greatest. No wonder all grown men wince at the thought of circumcision at ninety-nine," Leon quipped.

"Alright, so this is where it all comes into focus: All the promises given to Abram in his covenant were assembled on this day in his life when he could do nothing on his own, instead having to rely completely upon the ability of El Shaddai to accomplish what He had agreed to do for Abram." Leon paused for very long moment to permit what he had just revealed to settle in the thoughts of the people.

While he waited, he watched some of those who had been writing, suddenly stop and raise their heads in response to his pause. Off in the corner, one particular woman who had diligently been writing during the entire meeting suddenly squealed, "Yes! Yes! Yes! Yes!" threw her notepad in the air and jumped to her feet. As all eyes cast their gaze on her, the complexion of her face ran many shades of red while she tried to compose herself and sit back down.

"Finally!"Leon shouted enthusiastically. "Pastor Tim, there is your first convert," Leon exclaimed as he pointed at the blushing woman. "Look folks, what I'm saying here today is something that's not so much taught as it's caught. That's why I'm not offering chapter and verse citations. So you better get your nets up cause there is a lot more coming." he exhorted the congregation.

Chapter 8

"When Moses was introduced to God some 430 years later on the backside of the wilderness, He came to him as the 'God of Abraham, Isaac and Jacob.' The purpose of such a declaration was to inform Moses how the covenant agreement each of these generations walked under was still in effect with the children of Israel.

"I mention this because practically everyone forgets that the exodus from Egypt was a covenant matter established with Abraham. Every person who crossed the sea, who ate the first manna, or drank the water from the rock in the wilderness, did so, despite all their grumblings for three months, as recipients of a gift they did not earn, from a covenant they did not set in motion. The entire tribe was living through Abraham's covenant without knowing it would one day be described as God's grace.

"Let me draw your attention to a very specific matter involving Abraham's covenant and the children of Israel as they come into the wilderness. Look at the 32nd verse in the passage of Jeremiah 31," Leon said as he picked up his bible. "In the 31st verse God says He's going to make a new covenant, but look at this opening, '*Not according to the covenant I made...*' when He brought Israel into the wilderness. Now how many of you here can see how God's new covenant will not resemble the covenant from the wilderness?" Leon asked as he examined the faces of the people reading their bible.

"Does anyone know the name of the wilderness covenant spoken about here?" Leon inquired. There was a quiet shuffling of notebook papers and bible pages turning as Leon waited patiently. "Anyone even with a guess?" he pried. "I'm not making this too difficult am I? We're only dealing with three covenants today, Abraham's, the new covenant, and…"

"The Law!" came a young response from Leon's right.

"Yes!" exclaimed Leon as he spun towards the sound of the voice. "Who said that?" Leon asked as he pointed in the direction he heard the answer.

Sheepishly, a small hand raised in the air, as young William stood up. "I d-did."

"William! Good job, son. Keep it up!" Leon smiled approvingly. "Did everyone hear what William's answer was? The wilderness covenant is The Law. So God declares that the new covenant will not be like The Law.

"We're not done here though. Let's read some more out of this verse. '…out of Egypt; which my covenant they brake…' So God brings them out of Egypt and they break His covenant. What covenant are we talking about here? Those of you, who say it is The Law, raise your hands." Leon watched as a majority of the people raised their hands in the air. "Okay, how many of you believe it's the Abraham covenant?" A small amount of hands raised across the sanctuary. "Alright, how many of you have lost your hands? Raise your foot in response." Chuckles rang throughout the room.

"Well, those few who answered that the covenant they broke in the wilderness was the Abrahamic covenant, you are correct. I know, many recall the calf in the fire and Moses smashing the tablets as a result, but that was all a prelude to ratifying the demands of The Law which had already been given. They had already broken Abraham's covenant before this. How many of you are interested in knowing where and how they did it?" Leon asks as he scans the room and watches many hands rise in a tentative manner.

"I'll tell you what. Tim, I think that it's about time to call it done for the day," he said moving towards the pastor closing his bible. "I'll have to check my calendar for the next time I'm in your town," he responded coldly. Across the sanctuary could be heard loud moans and grumblings accompanied by shouts of 'No!' and 'Stay!' Stopping next to Tim's seat, Leon knelt down and slowly re-tied his shoelace while the audience's emotional cries grew louder. "Next comes the defining cut," Leon whispered just loud enough for Tim to hear who acknowledge with a nod of the head.

Standing to his feet, Leon looked over directly at Bill who was now seated very stoic in his chair looking unswervingly back at him. With a nod towards him, Leon began to raise his hand to the crowd. "Calm down. So you want to know what actions a body of one million people took because they thought it was better to live under The Law then live under grace. Or maybe it would be simpler to say, what is the one thing which will stop grace and move you into law?

"Go to Exodus 19 while I paraphrase what the setup. Three months have passed since they crossed the Red Sea and have now arrived at the base of Mt. Sinai. During these months, God has traveled with the children of Israel as a pillar of fire and cloud of smoke guiding them towards this mountain. He has provided food and water for them all along the way. He even aids them in the fight against Amalek who they soundly defeat.

"So when they arrive at the mountain, God calls Moses to come up because He has a message to deliver to the children of Israel. Pastor Tim if you could read verses 4 through 6 for us," Leon said as he handed him the microphone.

"Exodus 19:4. *Ye have seen what I did unto the Egyptians, and how I bare you on eagles' wings, and brought you unto myself. Now therefore, if ye will obey my voice indeed, and keep my covenant, then ye shall be a peculiar treasure unto me above all people: for all the earth is mine: And ye shall be unto me a kingdom of priests, and an holy nation. These are the words which thou shalt speak unto the children of Israel."* Tim handed the microphone back to Leon who stood beside him.

"God is love. This message is the greatest love message any people group could ever want to hear. Listen to grace speak out its love: *What I did to the Egyptians; I bare you on eagle's wings; brought you to myself; a peculiar, or better read as, a 'special' treasure; a kingdom of priests and a holy nation.* How many of you would like God to speak like this to you," Leon asked as he held his hand above his head and looked across the room at the small number of people who were following his lead.

"To secure all of this, all they had to do was obey His voice and keep His covenant. I'll state this again, simply to drive home the point. The covenant He is operating from here is Abraham's covenant, the same one which got them to their current destination. But they are about to back away from it, and it happens in verse 8.

"Moses goes down and tells the elders of the people all God has said to him. The people then answer together, *'All that the Lord has spoken we will do.'* Moses then went back to the Lord and told Him what was said. There it is. That was the breaking of the covenant," Leon said as he paused and looked intently at the faces which were rising up from their bible with questioning looks.

"Oh, I forgot, you're not Hebrew," Leon quipped. "If you study out this passage in the original language and syntax the phrase, 'we will do' literally means, 'we are well able to do.' Now I know this might not make much of a difference in your thinking of how this could break a covenant of grace until you hear it with all of its implications.

"All the Lord has spoken, we are well able in our own abilities, power and skill, to do what He requires of us as a people." Leon paused and watched the expressions of everyone soak up what he had just released. "Was it their power which parted the sea? Or how about their skill that brought water out of a rock? Or maybe it was their power which provided manna every day? But let's really drive this home: Was it their own might that overcame the Amalekites? They seem to think so. Why does someone need grace when they can do it all themselves? Does this make sense?" Leon asked. "So guess what God's response to their declaration is?

"This is my paraphrase of sorts. 'Alright, you think you can do this by your own strength. I'll make a covenant with you that will make you think twice about what you think you can do. It will be a covenant of works so stringent that if you miss just one little point in it, you've blown the whole thing. But I, because I still love you, I will place within the requirements a shadow of your eternal salvation which will keep reminding you just how difficult you've made this.'

"So God tells Moses to have the people prepare themselves and to not touch the mountain or they'll die. Just moments earlier there wasn't a problem being at the mountain, now it's deadly. They'd been traveling with God for three months and there never seemed to be a need to pay attention to these type of conditions before.

"They went from *'obey my voice'* to *'keep my commands and statutes;'* from resting in the presence to doing works in order to enter in; from a kingdom of priests to one high priest from only one tribe; from spiritual blessing made manifested to animal sacrifice demanded; from murmuring to people dying; from compassion to mercy; from right standing to unrighteousness; from a holy nation to unsanctified people; from a clear conscience to sin conscience; from a bride to a harlot; from the rock that quenches to the stone of offense. They had fallen from grace into the hands of The Law."

Stepping back a bit, he could see Tim's dazed face. Moving the microphone behind his back, he spoke to Tim, "You apparently never saw this one coming. How does your freedom feel my friend?" Tim smiled and slowly shook his head in agreement.

Leon looked out over the crowd and could see the same dazed expression on practically every person. "You people look like bull frogs in a hail storm. It's coming at you so fast you don't know what to do. Should I stop or go on?" Leon jokingly asked. "Go on!" came a loud chorus throughout the building. "But what about lunch? Isn't there a game on and a lawn to mow too?" he chided them. Again he was met by the chorus of, "Go on!"

"For far too long, the church has been functioning with an Old Testament mindset in a New Testament reality. What this means is that the light of truth has been replaced by the shadows the old covenant projected This is why there is a predominance of sin consciousness in almost every church body you go into today and it is keeping the people under its bondage.

"Listen carefully to what I'm about to tell you because many have taken this and said I was preaching something entirely different then what I said. The Father did not intend to give Israel the Law when they came out of Egypt. He was perfectly willing to continue on with them operating from the covenant which He made with Abraham. It was their decision to believe they themselves could do all which God required which created the Law as a factor in their relationship with God.

"Write this down: The Law was created to prove to Israel that they couldn't keep it. It was performance based worship at its best and a burden and yoke at its worst. Israel had to perform a multitude of works in order to stay in the perfect presence of God. The Law rewarded anyone who could perform the works of the law with the blessing of God in their life. However, no one was ever blessed by the works of the Law – they were blessed by the sacrifice which was required to cover their transgression to the Law.

"Once, every year, the high priest would come before the Lord and offer a sequence of sacrifices of a lamb, bull or goat which were to cover the sins from the previous year for the entire tribe of Israel. The blood from the sacrificed animal acted as a covering for the priest so he could enter the holy of holies. Without this covering, he would surely die in performing his duties. The priest knew how the offering would only last for a year, but it was what he was required to do, or perform, to keep God's wrath away from the tribe of Israel.

"Now I realize my explanation is general and I do this on purpose. First, almost all of you know a whole lot more about the fulfillment of the Law then you may want to admit. Whatever I left out, you have already embellished in your own thoughts. Second, I hit the high points simply because God said in Jeremiah that He was not going to create a new covenant like the Law. Why should I spend time on delving into the particulars of something God doesn't wish to visit again?

"Regrettably, for most believers, when God created a new covenant that took away their performance as a means to meet God's standard of righteousness and holiness, it caused a great rift in the time-space continuum. Unable to accurately define their stature according to statutes, they began to define what constituted acceptable behavior, performance, and eventually even attire. Suddenly the new birth based on the freedom of the Spirit became a reincarnation of religious traditions that made the word of God null and void. That's right. God's word is voided simply by your traditions.

"The dilemma is how all of our traditions are built on millennia of incorrect teaching. No one questions the traditions because they seem "right." But if they were wrong to begin with, no amount of "right" will undo the wrong they have produced. Now I say this as a backdrop to get you to think about the new covenant which you operate under.

"The new covenant was designed by God so everyone would know Him without the need of a teacher. The priests under the Law were the only ones who could teach people about God. However, their teaching never touched on the Fatherly nature which is the foundational characteristic of God. Jesus' mission on the earth was to reveal the Father. The requirements of the Law kept this facet of God hidden. Jesus turned the paradigm of the priests on its head. Never had a man in the community of Israel ever related himself to God within the context of a father/son relationship.

"This radical concept would lead Jesus into regular confrontations with the religious order of the day. On a number of occasions Jesus would almost be stoned for what the religious people saw as blasphemies against God. Consider the statement made by Jesus, '…I am the way, the truth and the life. No one comes to the Father accept by me…' Today, we don't see any significance in such a claim and readily acknowledge this verse in every salvation message we present.

"However, in the day when Jesus made this claim he slapped the entire religious order who had limited the access to an entire nation from the presence of God. In the temple service, the priests went through two of three doors as a part of their daily rituals. Only on the Day of Atonement would the high priest go through the third door. Each of those doors had a name: The Way, the entrance from the outer court to the inner court; The Truth, the entrance from the inner court to the holy place; and The Life, the entrance into the holy of holies. The priestly class, which only came from the tribe of Levi, understood the ramifications of Jesus' claim. For Jesus, or anyone for that matter, to enter through those doors would be a transgression of the Law. But with him being from the tribe of Judah, they recognized how only one other person from that tribe has ever walked through those doors into the presence of God lawfully. This was King David, and only an heir of his throne could rightfully make such a claim and not be held liable."

Leon looked intently out over the crowd. Many sat motionless and were transfixed in looking back at him. Looking down at his watch he slowly walked over towards Tim. "I've got one more vital point to make with these people and it is going to take some time to build," he said quietly to Tim. "How about we get back here tonight and drive this bus home?"

"Oh, yeah, y-yes," Tim stammered in bewilderment. "But we don't typically have night services."

"Good," said Leon with excitement as he patted Tim on the shoulder. "This is new ground for you and them," he said as he moved back up onto the stage. "I have so much more that you people need to digest but I can see how most of you are having a hard time just with what I've delivered this morning." Leon watched as many of the congregation began to act agitated by his statement.

"Here is what we're going to do. I'll be back here tonight beginning at 7:00 and we'll pick up right where I've left off." Leon watched as a vast majority of the members anxiously looked at Pastor Tim for agreement. "Pastor Tim has nicely provided me assurance that you will all more than eagerly attend this special message tonight. If you are unable to attend tonight, well I don't know what to tell you since it too will not be recorded. So I want to thank you for your time today. God bless each of you. See you tonight." Leon quickly gathered his material and briskly walked toward the door leading to the hallway passing Tim who was being swarmed by stunned members of his congregation. Quickly Leon moved down the hall and into Tim's office where he assumed his position behind the desk, looking out the window.

"Father, help him through this," he prayed as he watched the people begin to get in their cars to leave.

Chapter 9

Several minutes passed and Leon watched car after car pull out of the parking lot. From the expressions on their faces many of the people walked to their vehicles and drove off in a dazed stupor. Behind him Leon could hear the subdued sounds of people talking as they passed by the door to Tim's office.

"Yes, yes… I'll look into it," came the muffled voice of Tim approaching the door. Abruptly the door opened and Tim thrust himself inside and quickly slammed it. "What are you doing," he exclaimed as he pulled loose his necktie and threw his suit coat over the chair sitting in front of his desk. "We don't have night services here. Those people out there…"

"Are not the people you want here if they don't show up!" Leon quickly snapped back at Tim. "You want change to happen here, then you need to be ready to change yourself. Don't you ever forget how what has been done in the past here is what got you to this point. If you want my help, then take it as it comes no matter what manifestation it creates," Leon sternly responded.

Tim silently stood there considering all the alternatives he had. As each one ran through his mind he became more resolved to the path that he had taken. "I'm sorry, Leon. I never thought this would be so easier said than done."

"I know. It never is simple. Now you probably understand better why you could never deliver this message to these people. You have a vested interest in their lives. They look to you weekly for comfort and solace. That is not a bad thing unless they have stopped depending on the Father to be their comfort. I assure you that those seeped in sin consciousness have done this very thing. They are unjustly fearful of God. The relationship from a loving, caring Father does not exist in their thinking or actions. And the biggest thing you need to accept is how your actions have done this to them." Leon watched for any visible impact this last statement made on Tim.

Slowly Tim shook his head in agreement while he lowered his gaze toward the floor. "I know," he muttered weakly as he slumped down into the chair. Leon moved from behind the desk and stepped up behind Tim.

"Don't take it too hard, Tim," He said patting him on the shoulder. "We are often led by the sheep more than by conviction of our destiny. It happens to the best of us. Do you understand?" Slowly Tim shook his head as a sign of acceptance.

"I know this is easy for me to say but difficult for you to do. However, you need to forget what your members are saying right now to, and about, you. You need to focus on what is ahead – not tonight – but in the weeks to come. When I leave here you will have a completely different set of people here and they will expect you to answer their questions. Many of those questions will be centered around what you taught them in the past. Do not be fearful. Tell them the truth. If they can't reconcile their beliefs, then move on away from them. Don't ever go back to where they are at – always make them move up to where God is directing you.

"Yes, it may be lonely doing this but if you're looking for companionship, buy a dog. You can be friendly with people without having to be friends. Protect your God-given destiny by who you allow to come into friendship with you. Jesus had twelve disciples, but only three had direct access to him. And only one of those three had personal access to him. You will have this develop around you too. But it takes time and discernment.

"Look I've got to get some rest for tonight and you probably should too. I'll see you about 6:30. Don't worry about the usual warm up; I'll just kick it off, okay?" Leon said as he turned toward the door and quickly exited without waiting for Tim to answer.

As Leon walked down the hall toward the door to the parking lot, he glanced through an open door into the sanctuary. Seated in the dimly lit room was Bill leaning on his cane. Cautiously Leon entered the room and looked around to see if there was anyone else present. Not see anyone else, he softly walked across the room to where Bill sat keeping an attentive eye on Bill's lips to determine if he was praying. As he came within about ten feet of him, Bill lifted up his head so Leon could see that there were tear streams etched upon his face.

"Is everything all right Bill," he tenderly asked as he crouched down beside him.

Taking the handkerchief from his pocket, Bill wiped away the tears from his eyes and face. "What are you doing here?" he asked as he folded the handkerchief up and placed it back in his pocket.

"Bill there are two ways to answer that question. Out of respect for you I will forego the polite response and get right to the heart of the matter," Leon said looking Bill directly in the eyes. "Tim has asked me to come and dismantle all the false teaching which has permeated this body of believers for all of its years. That includes any, and everything you may be responsible for. Do you understand?"

For a long moment, Bill sat quietly looking back at Leon. "Thank you," he softly said. "I'll see you tonight." Slowly Bill rose from his seat and began to shuffle off towards the door. Leon watched him depart from the room before he began slowly walking towards the door himself.

"It's going to be a very interesting night," he exclaimed as he proceeded toward the parking lot and his car.

Chapter 10

There was an anxious anticipation in the air as members of the congregation shuffled eagerly into their seats. Most were a bit surprised to see Pastor Tim seated in the chair he had sat in earlier in the day right next to his wife. A few pointed at the podium which still lay on the platform. A hush fell over the crowd at 7:00 as Leon walked through the door. As he walked past Tim, he was handed the microphone, transfixed on his ultimate destination. Holding the microphone behind his back, he extended his hand toward Bill who had taken his seat in the precise location Leon had seen him just a few hours earlier. "Glad to see you Bill," he said as he shook his hand.

"I'm pleased to see all of you here tonight," Leon said as he turned toward the congregation and looked out at all who had come. "Tim, it looks like you got a few more here tonight than where we left off with this morning. Is there anyone here who wasn't here this morning? Raise your hands."

Scattered around the room there were several people who raised their hands in response to Leon's leading. "Good! Keep your hands up for a moment. Let me start this off with speaking to you people first. How many of you sinned this week? You can put your hands down as an answer." Leon watched as all the hands went down. "Tim. Tim, stand up and look at this," Leon eagerly exclaimed as he waved his hand across the room.

As Tim stood up and faced the room of people, Leon asked, "How many of you who didn't raise your hand sinned this week? Raise your hand." Leon and Tim watched as a few hands hesitantly rose across the room. "A pretty vast improvement wouldn't you say from earlier?" Leon questioned Tim. Vigorously shaking his head in agreement, Tim sat back down in his seat.

"Tonight I'm going to drive home one point. It is the foundation of Christianity which, unfortunately, most of the church has forgotten. I'll tell you what that point is at the end of the meeting if you haven't figured it out by then. For those of you who missed this morning's message, you'll have to get in touch with someone who was here since I purposely had them not record it," Leon said as he glanced around the room at the few people who were anxiously looking for a fellow friend. Pulling his bible from underneath the seat next to Tim, Leon paused for a moment before he settled into delivering his message.

"Turn with me to 1 John 3:8. Nope, let's go up a few verses. Go to verse four. Okay, uh, Pastor Tim. Could you read aloud verses four through eight?" he asked as he extended the microphone to him.

"Um, yeah, sure. 1 John 3, verse 4. *Whosoever commits sin transgresses also the law: for sin is the transgression of the law. And you know that he was manifested to take away our sins; and in him is no sin.* Verse 6; *Whosoever abides in him sins not: whosoever sins has not seen him, neither known him.* Verse 7; *Little children, let no man deceive you: he that does righteousness is righteous, even as he is righteous.* And verse 8;

He that commits sin is of the devil; for the devil sins from the beginning. For this purpose the Son of God was manifested, that he might destroy the works of the devil."

Leon reached down and took the microphone. "Thank you. Listen to what I'm about to say very carefully. According to verse eight, all of you who said that you sinned this week, you are a transgressor of the law and of the devil; so Jesus came to destroy you," Leon slowly and firmly said watching the surprised expressions on the faces of many of the people. "Does anyone disagree with what this says?"

Leon looked out across the sanctuary at the stunned appearance of the people as they tried to refute what they had just heard and personally read. "No takers? Okay, so let me ask you this, how many of you are of the devil?" Leon said mockingly. Carefully scanning the room with piercing eyes, Leon jokingly toyed with the people as he walked up and down the aisle. "Where are you, you pesky little devil? Come out right now." Many chuckled as he continued to diligently look around.

"What are you people laughing at? This is serious business," he snapped at them jokingly. As he resumed his position at the front of the room, he paused for a moment to allow the people to compose themselves. "Right now, God too is laughing. However, His reason is different from yours." Leon paused to see the reactions of the people to his statement.

"Who here, right now, is feeling a bit uncomfortable because the Father is laughing for reasons you don't know why?" Several hands gingerly rose across the room. "Good. Keep your hands up. Tim look at this," Leon urged as he patted Tim on the shoulder. Rising half way from his chair, Tim turned and looked at his congregation. "Stand up here with me, Tim, for a moment," Leon said pulling him out from his seat to his side.

"Those of you with your hands up, put your hand down if you believe God is laughing at your sin issue because He's going to get you later." A few hands lowered across the room. "Hands down if you believe He's laughing at you because you're not sure how to answer my questions." Many hands quickly lowered leaving still a large number of hands raised. "Hands down if you think He's laughing at you in general." A few more people lowered their hands. "Hands down if you think He's laughing at your sin."

Both men watched as no one lowered their hand. "Keep that in mind," Leon whispered as he leaned over toward Tim. "Okay last two chances. Hands down if you believe God is laughing at the devil." Again, both men watched as no one remaining lowered their hand. "You've got a real issue here Tim," Leon quietly exclaimed. "Okay, that's enough; put your hands down. Tim, you can take your seat again," Leon said as he began to pace in front of the people.

Leon searched through his bible while walking before the people. The silence only grew more oppressive. Occasionally he would look up, ponder some thought and then return back to thumbing through his bible. When he would reach the edge of the room he would promptly spin on his heels and resume his pacing back in the direction he had just covered. Suddenly, he stopped in his tracks and some in the audience gasped at the unexpected action. For several moments he stood there slowly nodding his head before he quickly spun around and faced the people.

"Keep your finger in your bible or mark the page in some way and turn to the book of Hebrews, chapter 10." Leon waited momentarily for the congregation to find their place before speaking. "Verse one reads:

'For the law, having a shadow of the good things to come, and not the very image of the things, can never with these same sacrifices, which they offer continually year by year, make those who approach perfect.'

"The law is where we have developed our predisposition to miss the mark God has set for each of us to reach. This missing the mark of God is rendered as the term 'sin' in the bible. There is no way around it. If there was no law there would be no sin. But that is for another time. For now I want you to diligently examine this verse.

"Notice how it states that the law was a shadow of good things to come but not the very image. How many of you are still waiting for this very image to appear?" Leon exclaimed while looking carefully at the congregation. Noticing how no one was responding to his question, Leon continued. "Now we all know how the law required sacrifices to be made when any one screwed up, right? But how many of you have every seen this result? This verse clearly claims that the sacrifices, which were made year after year, never made someone perfect."

Leon paused for a moment to allow the weight of his claim to be fully considered by the people. "We've done it also. Year after year we've read our bible, read the latest teaching books, memorized verses, sang the same songs, attended meetings, seminars, bible studies, home groups, on and on in attempts to become 'perfect'. Believe it or not, each one of these activities was a sacrifice of your time, and often your money. While they appeared to be 'godly,' they never made you more perfect.

"Okay, let's go to the next verse. Verse two states:

'For then would they not have ceased to be offered? For the worshipers, once purified, would have had no more consciousness of sins.'

"This freaks most of you out! Consider what this verse implies. If you were purified, there would no longer be any thought of sin. No more thinking about how you missed the mark of God in your life. Never ever thinking about how much of a screw up you think you are because you did something against God's word. This is pretty radical, don't you think?" Leon asked. Many of the people were beginning to nod their heads in agreement.

"Now watch this. Verse three and four claim:

'But in those sacrifices there is a reminder of sins every year. For it is not possible that the blood of bulls and goats could take away sins.'

"Year in and year out, everything they did to try to make themselves right before the eyes of God, according to the very instructions which He gave them to follow, only produced one result: It reminded them of their sin. How many of you have felt that way? I realize I'm repeating myself but year after year, service after service; altar call after altar call; baptism after baptism; worship service after worship service; prayer meeting after prayer meeting; bible study after bible study; daily devotion after daily devotion, and on and on and on and on. Nothing you do seems to be able to rid you of the scent of sin which permeates your very existence. Am I talking to someone here?" Leon entreated the people.

"This is the very core of the sin consciousness most church people operate from: The constant daily reminder of not being worthy. It does not help that most church leaders reinforce this same thinking from the pulpit at every meeting, weekly and/or daily broadcasts. Is there any wonder why the 'world' refuses to be associated with any of us? But look at these next few verses. Jump down to verse nine. It states,

'then He said, "BEHOLD, I HAVE COME TO DO YOUR WILL, O GOD." He takes away the first that He may establish the second.'

"He, in this verse, is Jesus. He came to do the will of the Father by taking away the first what? Anyone know what it was Jesus took away?" Leon asked scanning the room. "The Law?" came a voice from the back of the room. "The Law. That's a good answer; however, it's not just quite complete. Anyone else?" Seeing how no one was able to answer the question, Leon moved towards Tim. "Tim, could you read for us Luke 22:19 and 20?"

Tim took the microphone and turned the pages in his bible to the passage he was instructed to read. "John 22…no, I'm sorry. Luke 22, verse 19.

' And He took bread, gave thanks and broke it, and gave it to them, saying, "This is My body which is given for you; do this in remembrance of Me." Likewise He also took the cup after supper, saying, "This cup is the new covenant in My blood, which is shed for you. "'

Tim handed the microphone back to Leon. "This is at the last supper with Jesus. Notice Jesus claims that the cup which they took was the blood of a new covenant. Does this phrase 'a new covenant' have a familiar ring to those of you who were here this morning?" Leon watched many of the heads of the congregants nod in agreement.

"So the *'first'* in Hebrews 10:9 is the old covenant so the 'second', or new covenant, could be established. Does everyone understand that?" Leon asked the group. Again many of the people nodded their heads in agreement. "You do? Good. Now get ready for the fireworks. Before I read any further, let me remind you of this one fact. The new covenant was enacted two thousand years ago on the cross. The reality of this act on that fateful day is still operating throughout the earth today. It will still be operating tomorrow and the day after, and on and on into the eternal future." "Amen!" rose from a number of the congregants.

"So I mention the cross and your people finally give me an 'Amen'! Alright then, hopefully this will get you beyond that point," Leon smirked as he returned to his discourse. "Look at Hebrews 10, verse 10. It states the most amazing truth.

'By that will we have been sanctified through the offering of the body of Jesus Christ once for all.'

"Here is what I call 'the act of three words.' Notice the first three words, *'by that will.'* This connects us to the previous verse. It means whatever follows was the will of the Father in the establishment of the new covenant. So what happened?" Leon asked rhetorically. "It claims that we, you and me, have been sanctified by the body of Jesus. Now I know how everyone gets all puckered up when they read or hear the word *'sanctified.'* Look, let's quit playing church for a moment and just accept what the word means. It simply means purified, clean, spotless, without defect." Leon paused and watched the reaction which was rippling throughout the crowd.

"Let me reiterate that again. Sanctified means purified, clean, spotless, without defect. The offering of the body of Jesus on the cross made you purified, clean, spotless, without defect. Notice now the last three words in this verse, *'once for all.'* This act only occurred one time in all of history for everyone. It will never occur again. Not through any other person at any other time past, present or future." Leon continued to watch the agitation caused by revelation to increase in the people about him.

"So what does all of this mean? Go back to verse two for a moment and let's reread it in light of what you now know. It says that the worshippers, once purified, would have no more consciousness of sin. I know I'm going to catch flack from you religious nuts for saying this so just hit pause. The worshipper, once sanctified, purified, clean, spotless, without defect, would have no more…"

"YES!" came a loud shout from one of the people which was quickly followed by numerous shouts of "Amen, Praise God, thank you Jesus."

Leon grinned eagerly, tapped Tim on the shoulder and pointed at the crowd. "The sound of shackles falling off." Leon allowed the people to be caught up in the light of revelation for a moment. "Okay, all right. Let's calm down for a moment. There is still more to show you. Skip down to verse fourteen and we'll look at another amazing truth. Verse fourteen proclaims,

'For by one offering he has perfected for ever them that are sanctified.'"

More shouts of joy began to rise in the room. Leon waited a few minutes staring excitedly at the people. "Yes, that's correct. This verse clearly states you have been perfected in the one offering Jesus made. And how many years ago was this perfection made complete?"

"Two thousand years ago!" came a chorus of eager participants along with shouts of joy and clapping. Leon briefly glanced over at Bill to see his headed lifted up, his face streaming with tears and shouting out hallelujahs. Leon reached over and tapped Tim and directed his attention over towards Bill. A large smile cascaded across Tim's face as he witnessed the effect of the message upon Bill. Tim spun back towards Leon and gave a thumbs-up sign in appreciation.

"Okay, let's settle down. No need going all Pentecostal on me here. Before you know it you'll start dancing." Many joyously laughed at Leon's claim. "All right, let's get back to these truths. Is there anybody here who is older then Bill over there," he said pointing towards him. Seeing no one respond to his question, Leon continued. "Okay so then it would be safe for me to say that all of you have been 'saved' less than almost ninety years. Correct?" Leon asked rhetorically.

"However, the scripture we just read tells us how over two thousand years ago one offering was made which satisfied all sin over all time and made us perfect. So what happened to us that made us believe we weren't what the scripture says about us? Skip down a few more verses to Hebrews 10:24 and we'll look at something additionally. Verse 24 - actually I'm going to read from 24 to 27. Starting a 24, it says,

'And let us consider one another in order to stir up love and good works, not forsaking the assembling of ourselves together, as is the manner of some, but exhorting one another, and so much the more as you see the Day approaching. For if we sin willfully after we have received the knowledge of the truth, there no longer remains a sacrifice for sins, but a certain fearful expectation of judgment, and fiery indignation which will devour the adversaries.'

"So the *'assembling of ourselves'* is what most of us would call church. But let me ask you this: How many gatherings have you been to where the requirement of stirring up love, exhorting one another, good works, and so much more is the norm and not the exception? I know I haven't been to many in all my years. How can this be if it is clearly described here as what we are to do when we come together? I think it has everything to do with what follows in verse 26."

"*If we sin willfully...a certain fearful expectation of judgment...devour the adversaries.* I asked each of you today if you had sinned within the past week. I also showed you from 1 John how anyone who sins is from the devil. Do you all remember this?" Leon asked the crowd, waiting for their response. As many people acknowledge this, Leon continued. "Turn back to 1 John 3. This is the place I told you to mark previously. We read up to verse 8. With what you just heard about from Hebrews 10, I want you to look at this extremely vital verse which will help us to address this matter from Hebrew 10, verse 26. Are you there yet?"

Leon looked around the room at all the people studiously examining their bible nodding their head in agreement. "Let's go and read verse 8 again.

'He that commits sin is of the devil; for the devil sins from the beginning. For this purpose the Son of God was manifested, that he might destroy the works of the devil.'

"This is quite spectacular what I'm about to show you from this, so get ready. I want you to now read verse 9. It states,

'Whosoever is born of God does not commit sin; for his seed remains in him: and he cannot sin, because he is born of God.'

"How many of you are born of God?" Leon asked. Every hand raised in the air in answer to the question. "Are you sure? Earlier you told me that you were of the devil as indicated in verse 8. But now you're born of God. So which is it?" Leon chided them watching the perplexed expressions sweep across the room. "Come on people. It's one or the other. You can't be double minded in this because it tells us in the book of James that double minded people get nothing from God. You are either a sinner, a pawn of the devil, or born of God. Which is it?" Leon demanded.

Chapter 11

The air was thick with indecision. All around people were busily searching through notes and looking at passages in their bible. What had been a joyous event just moments ago had been transformed by a simple question directed at everyone's belief and their behavior. Leon had witnessed this before and he always found it hard to comprehend how such a simple question could send a person, even an entire congregation, into a tailspin of self doubt and looping angst. Yet he stoically stood there in the aisle watching people grapple with how they viewed themselves.

"Alright, just stop for a moment," he said with an air of annoyance. "Tim, you see this? This is the result of faulty teaching. These people can't even answer the most basic of questions about who they are. This is your responsibility," Leon sternly stated. Throughout the room the expressions of indecision switched to protection of a chastised friend. "Look at them," Leon continued as he waved his hand across the room. "They would rather sit in their pity party then admit they have been duped! This is what you get when sound teaching is corrupted by power hungry leaders!"

At this comment, Leon caught out of the corner of his eye a sudden movement. As he turned toward it, he was surprised to see Bill standing to his feet and sternly looking at him. As if he was a cork just released from pent up pressure, people around the room began to stand up with the same expression boldly emblazoned upon their face. Leon took a step back and looked down at Tim sitting in his seat. "Do you have anything to say for yourself?" Leon pressed as he extended the microphone him.

Tim sat there, eyes closed; rubbing his temples apparently ignoring what was happening around him. After a few moments, he slowly rose from his seat taking the microphone. With gradual measured steps he maneuvered himself next to Leon. A tremendous sense of love washed over him and tears began to well up in his eyes as he looked at the people who stood in his defense.

"Thank you, everyone. Please sit down," Tim began in a hushed voiced. People began to slowly sit down as he reached inside his jacket for a handkerchief. Wiping his eyes, Tim continued. "Leon was invited here for a reason. It's time you knew why. Most of my time in ministry has been spent here with you. There have been good times and times which yearned to be good. However, I have come to realize from the first day the heritage which came with this body was not where it should properly be. That was no one's fault you could pin it on. But it is my fault when I allowed it to continue without making a correction.

"The pressure from this has recently become just too overwhelming to me and my family. A few months ago after much searching and prayer, we decided we were going to call it quits and leave the ministry." A loud gasp rippled throughout the auditorium. A few women began to cry softly into their handkerchiefs.

"When I called Leon, my expectation was for him to come and just fill in the calendar until the day when we would leave. The Lord had other plans though. What Leon has said here today, not just tonight, but this morning too, can best be described as emergency surgery. The patient was in critical condition and it was vital to make incisions which would either lead to recovery or cause it to bleed out."

Reaching over, wrapping his arm around Leon and drawing him closer, Tim continued. "Leon, I want to thank you from the depths of my heart. Today you have fanned an ember I thought had been extinguished. I have found my true love again and I can't tell you what this means to me. If I leave this place tomorrow or stay, you have my deepest appreciation for what you have brought me. As for me, I know, again, that I'm born of God. So if you would, the patient still needs your attention. Make your final cuts," Tim proclaimed as he handed the microphone back to Leon and sat back in his seat.

"Thank you, Tim," Leon quietly responded to Tim. As he turned to look at the congregation he was met by many who were crying or staring off into space trying to stifle their emotions. Leon looked over at Bill who was resting his chin on his hands which wrapped around the crook in his cane. He too was staring out into space, tears streaming down his face. Leon turned back toward the crowd and waited a few moments to allow them to compose themselves.

"I don't know of a surgeon who enjoys cutting into a patient with no anesthesia. Yet I know that the Spirit of truth has made deep incisions this day which will bring great fruit and relief to many of you. There are however many questions left to be answered. So let's deal with where we left off and how my remarks to Pastor Tim got all of you so riled up.

"This entire passage out of Hebrews has to do with what happens when someone has a sin consciousness. Many, if not all of you, when you walked into this place tonight, suffered from this debilitating condition. Now understand this one thing: Your initial salvation experience did not produce this condition in you. I'm absolutely certain that when you first professed the lordship of Jesus in your life you were as happy and joyous as could be. Weeks might have gone by in this state and people would often ask you what had happened to you that made you so 'strange.'

"Regrettably, something transpired which you didn't readily have a defense mechanism against. Someone taught you how there is an accuser of the brethren who stands before God day and night leveling against you all the sins you have committed. Now everyone remembers their condition prior to salvation a whole lot more than their life after it. So this accuser dude was like a moth to the flame of your past craziness. So once the accuser was planted into your post-salvation experience, every message that mentioned the nature of sin, every altar call, every 'unholy' desire, came up on the radar of your thoughts and you began to believe that you're a saved sinner.

"Shoot you even have a scripture to back up your new belief and you repeat it often. 'I'm a sinner saved by grace.' Unfortunately, most of you don't have any clue what this verse is dealing with, but because it mentions sin and salvation together, you figure it just has to apply to you.

"Now this is where the torture of your form of salvation begins. You strive to try to feel the joy and happiness you did when you first got saved. But you know how you just did something which the accuser is now using against you. So when Sunday comes along you can't wait for an altar call so you can run up and get relief from the condemnation you've been experiencing all week.

"At that moment you feel better, so you determine how you'll guard yourself better by doing daily devotions in the morning. This you believe will keep the word of God in the forefront of your mind and prevent you from screaming at the idiot who just cut you off on your way to work. Not to be deterred further you begin attending a bible study on Tuesday. This keeps you satisfied by knowing you'll have several chapters to read throughout the week in preparation for next week's meeting.

"Wednesday is a mid-week service which curbs the sin consciousness through an altar call if you're really feeling convicted by the past three days. Thursday brings prayer group where you'll at least be able to relieve your guilt in quiet contemplation with others who are doing the same thing. Friday is when you meet with the drunken, drugged, pregnant, homeless, convict youth and young adults so your sin nature has someone to measure itself against and feel better at the end of the day. Saturday is a day just to yourself and you really don't want to think about all the things church is going to present to you the next day. So it's a freebie!

"Having just heard this, a sane person can only come away with two choices. First, you are a sin addict and church is your fix. Or second, your salvation is only evident on Saturday, which as weird as that sounds, could make you some member of a cult. But what is really scary is how you keep doing it week after week thinking somehow by doing it, your life will become better. It hasn't gotten any better though and you have resigned yourself to the fact that God is going to strike you dead any moment - especially on a Saturday."

Leon stopped to watch the reactions of the people. Many who had been incensed with him before had become resolved at how well he had just described their actions. Others were staring aimlessly towards the front of the room obviously overwhelmed by the amount of similarities in their lives they had just heard. Scattered throughout the room there were however those few who having heard their life's patterns, were eagerly waiting for what Leon would reveal to them next. These hardy people sat on the edge of their seats excitedly nodding their heads in agreement to every word which proceeded from Leon's lips.

"So let me confront this bad teaching about the accuser of the brethren. He is only mentioned in the book of Revelation under this title. You'll find him in chapter twelve. Now this is where most people get lost simply because they don't know how to read the entire book. So let me make it simple for you. In this chapter Michael and his angels kick Satan and his angels out of heaven. This isn't an event which will one day occur but it's a day that has already occurred.

"The teaching about the accuser gets all screwed up because people fail to take the verb tenses for real in the passage of verse 10. This verse states, *'And I heard a loud voice saying in heaven, Now is come salvation, and strength, and the kingdom of our God, and the power of his Christ: for the accuser of our brethren is cast down, which accused them before our God day and night.'*

"The phrase, '*is cast down*,' should be pretty self explanatory you'd think. But most teach how this is some event that will come sometime in the future. Even when you couple it with the phrase, '*Now is come,*' which can never be applied to a future event, the truth from this verse is somehow transformed from a present reality to a future wish. This one thing is what allows the power hungry leadership of a church to remain in control. If they have the devil at their beck and call through scripture, they can determine who in their congregation will submit to their brilliance.

"Tonight I have taken great effort to dismantle this erroneous teaching by showing you how God eliminated the position of the accuser of the brethren through the sacrifice of His son. If you're not certain how I did that then permit me to review what we spoke about tonight.

"First, just to make this straight, the accuser of the brethren was before God day and night telling him all about the sins you completed and how these sins could not permit you to be in the presence of God. Also, understand how before Jesus came, he also told God how the children of Israel weren't keeping the Law and therefore didn't deserve His blessing.

"We read tonight out of Hebrews 10:2 how the worshippers once purged should have no more consciousness of sin. Then from Hebrews 10:10 we discover how the offering of Jesus' body has sanctified, or made us purified, clean, spotless, without defect once for all. God told us in Jeremiah that under the new covenant He would remember our sins and iniquities no longer, and then in Hebrews 10:18, which I wasn't quit able to get to, we'll find this great truth: When sins are pardoned, or forgiven, there is no more offering for sin required. Finally, in 1 John 3:9 we find that the seed of God is inside of us and we can't sin.

"With your sins pardoned and purged; being clean and spotless before God who has no memory of your past, present, or future sins; and having the seed of God within you so that you can't sin, I can safely stand on the truth that the accuser of the brethren no longer has anything to hold before God about us. And if he can't accuse us, then the only person who can is ourselves. And the ex-accuser is more than eager to agree with any of you in this matter, since he's looking for something to do these days. Just remember he didn't instigate it, you did."

Leon paused to allow all he had just released settle into the thoughts of the people. "Realize this people: what I just spoke to you about is what the true gospel is about. This is what Paul and all the apostles taught to the early church. Everything I spoke on is what grace is all about. Grace is everything God did to bring you back into His family. I know some of you might disagree with this definition but I don't care. Take it up with Pastor Tim.

"God in his infinite wisdom created a path into His presence where our very own efforts could never work. Yes, that's right, never work. Christ is the end of the law. That not only means the old covenant with its laws and ordinances but your personal law. All a law represents is a way to be self-righteous by keeping it. So even if you don't follow the Law of the children of Israel as Moses declared it, as long you have some rule, order, or prescribed method to worship God and to come into His presence, it is a law Christ brought to an end. He did this because he is the only one righteous enough to be in the presence of the Father.

"However, even in this, God has made a way which simply comes by belief or what some call faith. Recall how Abram believed that God would provide him an heir. This act of believing in a promise from God is what made him righteous in the eyes of God. This is why God would come down to frequently visit Abram. This new covenant we function from is built around the same feature. We believe that Jesus completed all which was required to put us back into the household of God and we are declared righteous just as Jesus is.

"Please notice how I didn't say you had to do something special, perform some ritual, or drink someone's kool-aid in order to be righteous. There is not a single work you can do. All you must do is believe. This is why we are called 'believers' and not 'doers.'

"Now I know this claim just sent a number of your minds into overload. You've been told to be a doer of the word and how faith without works is dead. Well put those commands into the right perspective of grace and the doing is based on believing how God has provided everything you need in this life for godliness, while the work is offering thanks, believing the goodness of God will be made manifest to you. It's this simple. No programs or routines; only faith."

Leon stretched out his arm to look at his watch. "Oh my! I've really spent a lot of time on this tonight. I've got one more thing to address but honestly there just is not enough time available for us if you're planning on going to work tomorrow." Leon's claim was met by a chorus of moans of disagreement across the sanctuary. "Pastor Tim, since you've been so accommodating in opening this up tonight, let's shoot for wrapping this up tomorrow night at 7 o'clock." Leon said as he collected his materials and then handed the microphone to Tim.

"Surely," Tim responded with surprise rising from his seat. "We'll be here again tomorrow night folks. I can assure you it won't be a time you want to miss because we're not going to record it either," he said looking approvingly at Leon. Nodding his head in agreement Leon walked briskly over to meet Bill. "See you at 7 o'clock everyone," Tim announced over the din of people collecting their belongings and shuffling out of the sanctuary.

"I told you that I was here to correct some things," Leon said to Bill as he extended his hand to assist him in rising from his seat. "I hope you'll be able to be here tomorrow with this final piece."

"Yes, I'll be here," Bill replied. "You're doing a good work here. Thanks." he said as he patted Leon on the shoulder and began walking towards the door.

Leon spun around and saw Tim swarmed with people all asking questions. For a moment he thought about heading up the aisle toward the rear door, but realizing how leaving Tim to his own devices at this time might keep him from returning tomorrow, Leon walked over towards where Tim stood and pressed into the crowd grabbing Tim's elbow. "Tim, we need to let your wife know that we'll be a little late," he said pulling Tim towards the door.

"Uh…yeah…certainly, Leon. Thanks." Tim responded in a bewildered fashion. "I'll take all of your questions at a later time, folks. Thanks again. I've got to get to a meeting with Leon," Tim said pulling himself away from the people who surrounded him. "Thanks, they were getting a little overwhelming," he said catching up alongside of Leon.

"I know. It's going to be this way for a few weeks. Didn't want you to lose yourself in that just yet," Leon said as they entered Tim's office. "You okay with how things went tonight?"

"Yeah. Like I said, I've found my love again. I'm simply amazed at just how simple the gospel is. I see what you mean about power-hungry leaders able to turn something so simple into a works program to extend their own agenda. I think I stepped over into there a couple of times over the years, but now I know how it happens. Thanks for your assistance." Tim said as he took off his coat settled into his chair. "I don't suppose you already know we don't meet on Mondays here?" he chuckled.

"You do now." Leon laughed. "If things go well tomorrow, you may be doing it for a while. So you'd better get ready just in case. It's getting late and you should really get home to your family," Leon said turning towards the door. "It might be a good thing if you can get your wife to come tomorrow also. She might find things a whole lot different afterwards. See you at 6:30." Leon opened the door and walked out into the hall closing the door behind him before Tim had a chance to respond.

"Okay, sure," Tim answered behind the closed door.

Chapter 12

Leon could hear the muffled sounds of people talking in Tim's office as he approached the door to knock. He paused a moment to determine if by their tone it would be appropriate to enter. There didn't appear to be anything to heated happening so he knocked and opened the door slightly to see Tim partly seated on the edge of his desk. "Tim, am I interrupting anything important?"

"No, Leon. Come on in. I want you to finally meet my wife, Lisa," he said extending his hand toward his wife seated in the chair at the opposite end of his desk.

"Lisa," Leon said as he stepped into the room shutting the door. "It's a pleasure to meet you at last," he said extending his hand toward her.

Immediately Lisa jumped to her feet and threw herself past his hand and wrapped her arms around him. "Thank you, so much," she cried out as tears began to flow down her cheeks. "You have no clue what we've been through," she whimpered.

"Yes, I do Lisa," he calmly responded to her as he drew her closer to comfort her. "My wife and I went through the same situation many years ago. This is partly the reason why I'm here." They stood there for several moments until Lisa was able to compose herself and slowly drew away from Leon. Tim handed her several tissues as she stepped towards him. "Thanks," she whispered to him.

"I want you to know," she started as she blotted the running mascara from her tear streaked cheeks, "how last night was a message I have never experienced in all my years in church both as a pastor and a member. Something snapped in me and I have never felt this…this…free!" she exclaimed excitedly.

"That seems to be the most common response I get when I've done this in the past."

"How many times have you done this?" Lisa asked.

"I've been in the ministry for quite a while but this message I've done maybe a dozen times," Leon said pulling up a chair and setting himself down. "Most people who have years in 'church' seem to be the most impacted by it."

"I'll confirm that with you Leon," Tim interjected. "My phone hasn't stopped ringing all day with people telling me how what you said yesterday has completely transformed them. And many of these people were here years before we arrived!" Tim said excitedly.

"That's great to hear Tim. The ones who call tend to be the ones that stay. What about the ones you're not telling me about?" Leon pressed. "Are they the ones who didn't show up for the evening message?"

"There were only a few who indicated they had been to both messages and weren't happy where this appeared to be going. I think I spoke to maybe 10 or 12 people who were upset. Most weren't pleased how I would have you come in at all if we were planning on leaving anyway," Tim responded with frustration.

"Good. They weren't worth your time. So let's get back to the good things which are happening. Lisa, I'm not certain what involvement you wish to have in the future of this, but both of you, and your leadership team need to meet tomorrow and begin determining how things need to change within the operation of this ministry. You're not going to be able to go back to things as usual or you're going to have a full scale revolt here within about two weeks. It's hard enough making course changes when things are bad, but if you don't do it now, it will be like trying to ride a canoe over the wake of a speed boat. Something, or someone, is bound to go into the drink."

"I know what you're saying and I already set up a meeting tomorrow with my staff so we could do just what you've said," Tim said.

"Leon, I'm not certain what I'm going to do in this," Lisa stated. "I've got some…issues with certain…people. I'm not real comfortable right now being…"

"Lisa, you don't need to say any more," Leon interrupted. "I fully understand. My wife went through the same thing at our church too, on more than one occasion. I know whatever the difficulty is it will work itself out. Honestly, the best thing for right now is for you to really just stay in the background and support Tim. It is going to get pretty weird around here for a few months while the dust settles. He's going to need someone who isn't in the thick of it to keep him centered. Do you think that you can do this for him?" Leon asked in a fatherly manner.

"Y-yes," Lisa stammered as tears once again began to flow down her cheeks.

"That's good. Look you two, I'm here to provide any help you need. But once I'm gone, you've got to stick together through whatever comes. Your faith will be tested in ways you can't imagine as old friends drop by the way side and begin to say things you wouldn't believe possible. Even new friends will surprise you with their…what should I call it…their stuff. But you will make it through, I know, even if you don't think it will be possible for a time.

"Just remember that you're not here to help everyone, just those who are called to work alongside of you. Your work, your mission, your purpose is to help them achieve the greatness which was placed within them. This is how you will complete the desires which have been placed within your heart. Many will look at what you're doing as being completely backwards from how they were brought up in the church, but pay no attention to them. They are only there to provide you with confirmation that you're following the right path. Who you lose is not as important as who you retain."

"Leon, Tim told me you call this the forbidden message. Why is that? I haven't heard or seen anything which would give it such a reputation," Lisa inquired.

"Lisa, when a church is going in a direction which is not the way of truth, the last thing the presiding pastor of that church can do is come and tell them they are off. He loses all credibility with the people should it ever occur. This is why the message of truth is forbidden. Not that the content is, but the person who delivers it is forbidden. Many will think what they are hearing is 'suspect' the moment you use the term 'forbidden.' This is a good thing believe it or not. What it does is begin the weeding process of removing those who are so religious minded that they might stay if you gave it some more generic name.

"Tim could never give this message here. All of your people have seen him over the years as the person who has faithfully guided them. When someone like me, who doesn't know the structure or cliques in a congregation, comes in and begins to speak like I have, there are two choices the leadership has to make: dispel all that was said, or embrace the message. I've seen both sides of the coin in this drama and trust me, despite the pain it might cause in the short term, embracing the message always has greater rewards attached to it.

"I haven't revealed any new 'inside' information in this message. I have simply offered the gospel in a format that closes all the avenues of escape religious people want to take to bring all of us back under the works which Christ clearly destroyed. It is quite possible that I might not close all those openings tonight but you will be ready to handle any which might arise from those who could possibly bring them up just with what I've given you.

"However, I want to make one thing clear. When a congregation becomes more sin conscious rather than God conscious they find themselves also becoming a 'needs center.' Everyone's needs start flowing out as a result of their introspection on the alleged sin they are focusing on. What I've seen time and time again is that the ones who rush the quickest to the altar are the same who flood the prayer request lines or ask for the benevolence funds every month.

"What this message will do is drive these people to make a choice between living the truth and becoming free or leave to find some other body they can feed off of. I know this sounds harsh, but ultimately it become their choice to make. Those who embrace the truth of the message will find their lives dramatically changed for the better. They will be your strongest defenders of what God has done through your ministry. Those who can't bear the truth will slink away because they soon discover you don't cater to their way of living.

"If you really want to discover who these people are in your congregation try this test. Don't do an altar call for about a month. During that month watch who keeps approaching you and your staff asking you to pray for them about an issue they should be able to handle in their own ability. Press them to step up and take responsibility first based on all they have been taught from the pulpit. Show them how the message which was preached within the last week or two directly applies to what they are facing. If they get all dejected and pouty, then watch them carefully. These are likely candidates to leave your fellowship. I know this this might seem like a radical approach, but the results will be amazing."

"I'd say it's radical," Tim interjected. "There are a few people I can think of right now who have been coming to the altar more times than I can remember. It's like they have a standing reservation there! They are the biggest drain on the time of each of us on the staff. I've never known how to address this correctly without telling them out of frustration to just leave the congregation."

"Been there and done that," Leon quipped. "Look, our school systems in this country are designed to move children through various levels of their lives. Churched should do the same thing. The trouble is we've permitted saved people thirty, forty, even fifty years in the faith to remain in their diapers and suck on their binkies. Show people how you're no longer going to be a preschool for God and you'll see a dramatic shift in the type of people who are attracted to your message."

Leon looked up at the clock on the wall and jumped to his feet. "Oh my goodness! We better get out there. Don't want to be late for this last session," he said as he rushed toward the door and held it open for Tim and Lisa. "Tonight is when all of this comes into alignment," he said excitedly as he followed behind them, closing the door.

Chapter 13

The last wisps of the worship music were still resonating through the sanctuary as Tim, from the main floor, approached the music stand which was to be the podium for the night. Behind him, on the stage, still lay the sanctuary podium which had been tossed during the Sunday morning service. Tim had felt it needed to remain there as a symbol for the new direction which things were headed.

Still enraptured by the strains of the worship, Tim lifted his head toward the ceiling and closed his eyes gently swaying side to side to a rhythm that had become internalized from the sound they had been absorbed in. Moments passed before he opened his eyes and looked out over the congregation, which like him, were enjoying their time of worship.

"It has been a long time since we've experienced this...this...closeness," Tim spoke with reverence. "I don't want to spoil this atmosphere so if you could quietly take your seats, being mindful of His presence, we'll proceed." Tim watched as the people silently retired to their seats, many of them wiping tears from their face.

"Before I invite Leon back up here to bring the last of his message for us," Tim began, "I want to take this time to extend to him my sincere gratitude for what he has done here, not only these past two days, but also all the time you've taken to work with me since I called you, what two months ago?" Tim said looking at Leon nodding his head in confirmation. "You have pulled me from a very dark place and I, no, Lisa, my family and I, we want you to know just how much we appreciate what you have done. If all this folds up tomorrow," he said waving his arm across the sanctuary, "I would still be honored to call you a great friend. Thank you. So please come now and release what you have for us," Tim said as he extended the microphone toward Leon.

As Leon rose from his seat, Lisa, who sat next to him, patted him of the back offering her thanks too. Approaching Tim to take the microphone, he was greeted by Tim's emotional embrace. "Thanks Tim," he said as he wrapped his arms around Tim and drew him closer, patting him on the shoulders. "It is an honor to call you friend too." After a few moments the men parted and Leon approached the podium. After he placed his bible and notebook on the stand, Leon turned and looked at the podium on the stage for a long moment before turning to face the congregation.

"Thank you, Tim," Leon began. "Looking out over this group tonight I am reminded of the story of the Samaritan women at the well who met Jesus when she came to get water. The bible says that she, after speaking to Jesus, left her water pots behind and went into the town telling everyone to come see the man who told her everything she ever did. Jesus ended up spending two days there with those people out of this one encounter. If you're here tonight because someone in this congregation spoke to you about what happened here yesterday, could you please stand up so we can recognize you."

Scattered around the sanctuary, one by one, people stood up as instructed. "Tim, come look at this," Leon said excitedly pulling him up by his arm. Tim looked out at the people standing and grinned in approval, patting Leon on the back. "Those of you seated, please give these wonderful people a handclap of appreciation for coming here tonight. You may be seated."

Leon waited for a few minutes to allow the applause to die down before he began. "There must be about twenty percent more here tonight than last night. Thank you for coming. I trust you'll get something out of this message.

"We have been dealing with the sin consciousness which plagues most churches and the non-believers they support. If you want to know what we covered in the two sessions we held yesterday, you're going to have to find someone who was here since we intentionally did not record it. This will be the case tonight too.

"As a demonstration of what we've covered from the past messages, I want to ask you newcomers a simple question. How many of you sinned during the past week? Lift your hands high and remember you're among friends so we won't tell anyone?" A few snickers trickled throughout the people while cautiously a number of hands rose in the air. "Remember lying is also classified as a sin," Leon joked.

"Okay, put your hands down. I want you who raised your hand to find someone who answers this next question. With show of hands from the congregation, how many of you can't sin?" Across the sanctuary hands briskly shot up into the air.

Leon smiled broadly as he scanned the room. As he reached the end of his viewing he landed upon Bill seated in his same place, a great smile across his face, his arm waving in the air.

"Before you visitors get all freaked out, thinking this is a cult, I've spent an entire day with these people getting them to understand the truth of God's word regarding this matter. They have all answered correctly. This is why I told you to go and find one of them and have them tell you what the truth of the gospel truly says. When they show and tell you, it will bring further clarity to them too.

"Before I get started here I want to say one thing to all of you. It is no stroke of chance how you are here tonight to hear this message. Despite the daily trajectory each of our lives takes, this is the one night and the one place, where the will of the Father will be displayed in all of our lives. I know some of you might think you came here on your own freewill and that's okay. You'll probably discover differently a bit later. Because tonight, this is all about the Father.

"When Jesus walked the earth he had one mission. Display what it was like for man to have a relationship with God as the Father. His first recorded words at the age of twelve recorded in the second chapter of Luke tells us he knew that he was supposed to be about his Father's business in the temple. What is important here is it wasn't in the marketplace where Jesus mentions his relationship with the Father, but in the place where the greatest impact should have been understood in all of Israel – the temple priesthood.

"In those days being about the father's business meant the heir would be learning about how to conduct the family business. This business would be transferred to the heir upon the death of the patriarch. Jesus wasn't learning the carpentry business of Joseph in this depiction. He was astounding the religious people with how much he knew about the eternal Father in what the leadership knew was the heart of Israel.

"Sin is a heart issue. Proverbs 20:9 says, *'Who can say I have made my heart clean, I am pure of my sins.'* We also find in Proverbs 4:23 how we are to keep our heart with all diligence because out of it are all the issues of life. Samuel tells us God looks upon the heart of man rather than his appearance. Jesus enlightens us that out of the abundance of the heart the mouth speaks, and where your treasure is, there your heart is also. He also said how a good man out of the good treasures of the heart brings forth good things, while an evil man out of the evil treasures of the heart brings forth evil things.

"So when Jesus is speaking in the temple about the Father, he is determining what the heart condition is of the leadership of the people. How you feel about yourself is a direct reflection of how you determine what God has done in your heart. So why am I talking about the condition of your heart? Let me demonstrate with this little test. Raise your hand if you feel right now you can walk right into the holy of holies and stand in the presence of God."

Leon watched as a very few number of hands hesitantly rose into the air. He scanned the crowd and finished by looking down at Tim and Lisa sitting next to him whose hands weren't raised either. Shaking his head in disbelief, he tugged on Tim's arm and motioned with his head to rise up. Tim rose and looked out over the congregation. Moving the microphone behind his back, Leon moved closer to Tim. "Get a good look at these people with their hands up. They are your core leaders in what is coming. I hope at least one of them is on your staff."

Leon allowed Tim to get a good look at his people and then he extended his hand toward Tim's seat to signal for him to return there. "I am happy to see some of you know who you are. As for the rest of you who did not raise your hand, I can bet there is in the inside of your heart some doubt as to whether you would survive such an encounter. Am I right?" he asked watching several heads nod in agreement.

"I can also trace this doubt to a fear which you have about the awesome power of God that blows up anything which isn't as holy as He is. In fact, this fear comes from the stories we've been taught about the priests who went into the holy of holies on Yom Kippur to make the yearly sacrifice for the people of Israel. If the offering wasn't accepted, we've been told the priest would be slain right there and would have to be pulled out by a rope which was tied around his foot.

"Stories of this sort are what put many people in doubt of their ability to stand in the presence of God. The story may be factual, but is it true; or put another way, is it the truth according to you today? There is a difference in our case here. The facts are priests died when the sacrifice wasn't accepted before God. The truth is this always occurred before the new covenant; it hasn't occurred since the new covenant was instituted.

"I said yesterday how the trouble most believers have is they live their new covenant life from an Old Testament mindset. Recall from our scripture in Jeremiah 33 how God stated quite clearly He would write His commandments upon the tablets of our heart in this new covenant we have with Him. Practically everyone believes those commandments are the same ones the people of Israel were given, and still live by. But this isn't the case. God clearly stated in this same passage in Jeremiah 33 how the new covenant would not be anything like the old.

"In the old testament God would travel with the children of Israel in a tabernacle which they constructed each time they moved. This was constructed from a pattern Moses received from the heavenly temple. Centuries later David would construct another tabernacle that didn't have all the detail of Moses' pattern. Its pattern simply relied on the service of priests giving continuous praise and worship to God. David's son, Solomon, took the plans which David drew up and constructed a temple that blended both patterns from Moses and David together. When this new temple was dedicated, the presence of God's glory so filled it that the ministering priests fell over from the weight of God's glory. But this didn't last long in the history of Israel. It took Stephen, centuries latter, to remind the religious leaders of his day how in the heavenly pattern God doesn't reside in a temple built with hands.

"In each of these depictions, it represented a heavenly pattern which is now fulfilled in us. The apostle Paul reminded the people of Corinth that they were the temple of God and how the Spirit of God dwells within them. This is a new covenant reality. Each one of us, as believers, is the holy of holies where the Spirit resides. Those of you who couldn't raise your hand must recognize that you are declared holy by God. There is nothing, and no one, who can remove this declaration. The Spirit will not live in a dirty temple. So with the Spirit of God residing in you, you can't think you're impure or dirty – ever! You are at every moment well able and expected to stand in the presence of God."

Leon paused for a moment to allow this statement to lodge in the minds of the people. He watched as the countenance of many of the people relaxed in their new-found identity.

"Remember how I said that sin consciousness is a heart issue. Let me have you consider this question: Which is more powerful, your sin or God's love?" Leon waited for a few moments to allow the people to consider his question. "I believe - and let me state that this is just my belief - but until you come to a revelation of God's love, your sin consciousness holds more power over you than God's love. This means that despite what the word of God says about who you are in relation to Him and the vast love which He has poured out for you, your thoughts will surrender to your old self rather than to truth. This is why Paul tells us to renew our mind and not be conformed to the things of this world.

"I was just reminded of a story that is a slight trail off of where I going but you can all use a rest to a degree. I have a friend who is a contractor. A few years ago he found in his community an abandoned farm house which was pretty run down. The years had taken a toll on the inside because holes in the roof had allowed water to ruin a lot of the finishes. He acquired the property with the intent of remodeling the house and reselling it. As he prepared to tackle the job, a neighbor asked my friend if he was interested in constructing a new house for him on the same property which could complement the architectural style of the old house.

"Since the lot was large enough to build another structure without really encroaching on the existing structure, my friend agreed to construct a new house for this neighbor at the same time he was remodeling the farm house. My friend told me how the two projects were a great experience for his crew because when they were delayed on one house they would work on the other. This type of project kept all of his crews fully occupied for about 12 months from start to finish.

"After both were completed the new house looked nearly identical to the original in its architectural style: Wrap around porches; two stories with dormer windows on the front and back; central chimney and two side chimneys; and windows which looked just like the original. The inside had all the modern conveniences with surround sound system in the family room, stone counter tops in the kitchen, internet connections throughout the entire house, zero clearance gas fireplaces, the latest in heating systems and plumbing components, on and on.

"The remodeled house had a number of the same features but because of the nature of the structure of the house there were a few things that they just couldn't replicate from the new house. He told me how they had to go with a completely different heating system because of how the old heating system was positioned in the house. The same thing happened with the plumbing for a couple of the bathrooms since it originally only had one bath down stairs in the back of the house. They also ran into a number of issues trying to work with the electrical wires in the house. The building departments made them upgrade the wiring in a number of rooms so the house was up to code. The chimneys had to almost be entirely rebuilt and new flue liners placed in them. The worst was the roof and the water damage it created. There were whole rooms which had to be taken down to their studs just to get all the water damaged materials removed. A number of rafters had to be replaced because they were rotted throughout.

"As a side note, what I found to be an amazing thing about these two buildings is they almost cost identically the same to construct. Most of the costs for the remodeled version were simply because it took longer to finish than the new one.

"The new house actually was a gift from the neighbor to his wife, who never knew it was hers until the day he handed her the keys. They occupied it for almost an entire year before there was a serious buyer for the remodeled version.

"Finally, it came time to sell the remodeled one. My friend told me the one drawback in selling the remodel had to do with the water damage issues in the structure. Even though they had removed everything that was affected and treated the remaining wood for mold, he said every time the humidity rose outside, there was always a faint smell of mold which still lingered in the house. They never could tell where it was and they went through the house with a fine tooth comb treating everything, but he told me once the smell has penetrated the structure it's always going to be there in some degree.

"My friend told me he only was able to sell it once he had obtained a certificate from a laboratory who had conducted a series of tests looking for any active mold spores and the health department for the community signed off on it. He also had to take out an insurance policy for five years to cover any expenses which could possibly arise over the time frame should mold reappear in the areas he repaired. He said that that act of insuring the work was the scariest thing he had ever done because he knows he did everything correctly but he has no idea what the occupant of the house is going to do to it and then later claim it was his fault. He is still waiting for the time frame to be completed and worries about it more and more every day.

"So what does this story have to do with what I've been speaking about? Paul says God has made us to be new creations. He is not in the remodeling business. You are fully updated to permit the holy trinity to reside in you. They have everything they want inside the new creation you have been made into. There is not the least faint of a whiff of decay in you as a new creation. As the temple of God you are fully wired with the most advanced technology to keep you in constant communication with the Father.

"The trouble most people have with this reality is that they look in the mirror and, by all appearances, they look the same as they did before they got saved. However, since they never get beyond the outer appearance they are never aware of what went into the making of the new creation. They never see the great efforts taken to make the creation able to capture and sustain the weighty glory of a majestic creator. They overlook how they have the most advanced power system known to mankind while groping around for the 'switch' to turn it on. They know nothing of the eternal insurance which envelops all the acts of God in this creation. And most importantly, they miss the fact how the new creation is a bride gift designed to be a compliment to the surrounding community."

Leon paused for a moment to reach for a bottle of water that sat on the edge of the stage. He watched the congregation absorb what he had poured out to them as he drank from the bottle. Looking about the congregation, Leon asked, "Is young William here? The boy I spoke with yesterday." A shuffling rippled throughout the group as heads turned looking for the lad. From the back of the room a faint cry arose. "Here I am."

"Come down here for a moment, William. I want to ask you a question." Leon waited as the boy pushed his way through the row of people. Once he reached the aisle he quickly ran to Leon. "Good to see you again. Is everything going well with you?" Leon said kneeling down to meet the youngster.

"Yeah. My dad got to come tonight," he said with glee. "It's his night off work."

"Great! Look William, I want to ask you a question. You can answer it if you want but if you don't, that's okay. You can go back to your seat and we'll just go on with things. That okay with you?"

"Sure."

"William, do you believe Jesus lives in you?" Leon asked.

"Yes, I do," William proudly exclaimed.

"Great! Do you know where he lives in you?" Leon inquired.

"That's easy. In my heart," William beamed with confidence.

"That's right, in your heart. Thanks William. You can go back to your seat now," Leon said patting him gently on the shoulder. Leon rose as William happily skipped back up the aisle.

"Ask any child, just as I did to William, and they'll respond the exact same way – Jesus lives in our heart. Now recall how I said sin consciousness is a heart issue. Have you ever considered how it's possible for Jesus to occupy a place in each one of us which is so associated with sin? All you have to do is look through the bible and you'll find verse after verse which clearly describes the condition of the heart of man as wicked, evil and deprived. These really only reinforce our question of how Jesus could reside there, right?" Across the room heads nodded in agreement.

"But let me show you something. Up to this point I've been isolated on the passage out of Jeremiah 33 dealing with the new covenant. There is however a parallel passage found in Ezekiel too. Turn with me to chapter 36," Leon said grabbing his bible and thumbing through the chapters. "Let's see where to start. Yes, there it is. Let's start at verse 25 and go to verse 27. It reads:

"Then will I sprinkle clean water upon you, and ye shall be clean: from all your filthiness, and from all your idols, will I

cleanse you. Verse 26. *A new heart also will I give you, and a new spirit will I put within you: and I will take away the stony heart out of your flesh, and I will give you an heart of flesh.* And finally verse 27. *And I will put my spirit within you, and cause you to walk in my statutes, and ye shall keep my judgments, and do them.*

"What's interesting about these two people, Jeremiah and Ezekiel, is how they both are speaking about a new thing God is going to do but they are in different locations during the same period of time in Israel's history. What I want to call your attention to is the statement Ezekiel makes in verse 26. ... *I will take away the stony heart out of your flesh, and I will give you an heart of flesh.* What is the purpose of this new heart of flesh?" Leon asked rhetorically. "It says right there beforehand. To house the new spirit God is going to place within you.

"Consider how God already knew we have a stony heart and there is no possible way for it to suitably sustain the environment needed for a new spirit. So when you became a believer, there was a spiritual heart surgery done on you which took away the old heart you possessed and gave you a new one that is perfectly designed to house a new spirit. Nothing in the natural was evident, but it surely happened in the spiritual realm.

"Colossians furthermore tells us how at the same moment there was a circumcision made without hands which was performed on you. This was in answer to the prophetic plea of Moses made in Deuteronomy where he cries out that the hearts of the children would be circumcised so they would love the Lord God.

"So here is where the rubber meets the road. Either you believe God made you a new creation or you've just been remodeled. If you're a new creation this means you believe Jesus is the last sin offering; you recognize that his offering has forever perfected you and sanctified you or made you holy; you know his blood has purged your conscience from dead works; you realize God does not remember any of your sins past, present or future; and your identity in Christ is signified by a new circumcised heart which has written upon it the law and commandments of God. These are but a few of the distinguishing factors of a new creation a remodeled version of 'you' does not possess.

"Now what is vital to living as a new creation is how you must constantly recall how all of this was accomplished over two thousand years ago and it will continue to ripple throughout the expanse of time up until Jesus returns. This means that tomorrow you will still be just as new as you were today and yesterday.

"In the book of James we are introduced to the royal law of God's kingdom. It is simple and actually the only one written down for us to collectively follow. It states that we are to love our neighbor as ourselves. Recall how I said whenever there is a law for us to follow the enemy will come and try to tell us we shouldn't do it. Well here is the enemy's argument for why we shouldn't follow the royal law: If you do this, you will be like God." A chuckle rose across the room.

"Sound familiar? That is the same line of thought he gave the woman in the garden. But consider this: A new creation, who is holy and greatly beloved, which houses the Holy Spirit on this earth, is well able to love their neighbor since the heart is now congruent with the God of the universe who is, according to 1 John, love personified. If you say I can't love myself, you forget that it's not you who lives but Christ who lives in you. Surely you can love Jesus and then love your neighbor as Christ loves them, right?"

Looking around the room Leon could see a number of the people were picking up on the message he was proclaiming. "Understand this people, God has claimed that all the issues of life spring from the heart. He simply wants to be in the center of where all the action is. From this spot He will be able to guide you through all the stuff which comes at you. You unfortunately block His ability to help any time you focus upon an event that reminds you of a sin. How do I simply put this; there is no more sin because Jesus took care of it forever! If you don't believe me, then go look at the passage in Galatians 5 where Paul describes things like adultery, theft, murder, and a whole range of things we've known to be sin according to the Old Testament. Paul calls them the works of the flesh. Not sin, but the works of the flesh.

"Your flesh was crucified on the cross with Jesus. Those works hung there with Him. This is what a sin offering is for – to provide remittance for a transgression. Since Jesus is the final sin offering, there can be no more sin. Otherwise, there would have to be another sacrifice to cleanse its effects. But Jesus cleansed everything for all time.

"I want to end this message with this one last thought. There is not one thing you can do to add to the work the Father did to bring you back into His family. You can't praise more, read more scripture, do more devotions, prayer more fervently, share your testimony, attend more conferences, believe any stronger, fast more often, read one more spiritual book, and yes, even hear one more sermon in order to get something you think you don't possess. God has given everything to, and for you. He has done this from the very core of His character which is called love. The great vastness of this love is all Paul says we need to focus upon in order for us to be able to comprehend the fullness of His kingdom.

"The next time you hear someone tell you how you need to 'do' something to make you more holy or to please the Father, run away as fast as you can. That person is bound to a law which leads to death. Jesus came so you may have the God-kind of life and life more abundantly. Trying to follow a set of rules or procedures, either man-centered or from the law, will not lead you to the life He gave you through His sacrifice. The Father simply asks you to believe His son has done for you what you could never, again I say, could never, ever have done on your own. That type of belief is what is called faith and it pleases your Father.

"Jesus tells us in order for these things to be understood we need to be born again. Now I'm not going to go down that worn out path you've all heard about this time in every sermon. I want to make a point. The book of Romans clearly states how through one man, Adam, sin entered the world. We are all born from Adam. Each person in the world is a carrier of his sin DNA. You are born into it and there is nothing you can do to remove it. It will forever keep you away from God. This reality is your sin consciousness before salvation.

"When you believe in the finished work Jesus did on your behalf, your spiritual death and resurrection brings a new life to you which voids the DNA of Adam and establishes the DNA of the Father in Christ within you. Your new birth in the spirit realm signifies you as a child of God, an inheritor of the promises of Christ.

"Paul is very clear about our new nature. We live in a physical body but we inhabit heavenly places right now. Not some day to come, but right now. This is why we must renew our minds. If sin consciousness kept God away from you in your old nature, your thoughts need to adjust to who you are now in your new nature. There is no sin in heaven where you reside, just as there is no sin recognized on earth where you are right now sitting. Jesus has taken care of all of that, period. So get your mind to accept it.

"And if this seems impossible, remember this: God has forgotten all of your sins. He does not know they ever occurred. If you think that on the final Day of Judgment you will be hauled before his throne and a door will open which reveals all the sins you've committed or that some video is going to play showing all your past, think again. He does not know that you sinned. There isn't a secret stash of sin memorabilia they keep around on each of us. You're clean, spotless, pure, and forever will be. So get used to it.

"Jesus himself even declared in John 3 that if you believe in him you wouldn't be judged. If you really want to be technical about all this sin consciousness, if you really think you're a sinner, even after all I've said to you over the past couple of days, then accept this as the full measure of God's truth on the matter. The only sin which remains in this world, the one and only sin which the Holy Spirit convicts anyone on is this: You don't believe in Jesus," Leon forcefully said.

Leon pause for a long moment to allow the gravity of his last statement make its fullest mark. "Did you hear what I said? If you're feeling guilty about any sin in your life since the day you've been born again, then I would have to question whether you have even been saved ... AT ALL!" he yelled out into the congregation.

A wave of surprise shook the crowd as he delivered his last words. Leon watched the countenance of many of the people gently relax as they realized the magnitude of his declaration. For the first time he was witnessing through their posture the manifestation of accepting the truth which had been working in their lives all along.

"I have been very purposeful in the messages I have delivered here. However, I realize by doing this, I will have raised a number of questions which I might not have answered in the time I've had. This is good for you and your pastor. Questions spur inquiry into the deeper truths God is waiting to reveal to you. It also places a responsibility on your pastor to properly study in order to answer your questions in the same spirit they were created within you.

"I'm charging each of you not to accept any answer from him, or anyone in leadership, which moves you back into the arena of the law. I know this will put many of them on the defensive right off, but they need to pull up their britches and start functioning for real in what God has called them to do. If any of you takes exception to what've I just done, the door is right over there. You will find how there are any of a number of churches across this nation which will take you and plug you into their system of behavior modification and you'll never have to push yourself into the deep things of God. But if you want to be challenged in your faith for the truth, then I can't think of a better place to be then right here in the midst of all the turmoil I've intentionally created by not compromising on the truth of God's word.

"Now that I've delivered this truth to you, there is a great responsibility hanging around you. How you respond will either be seen as belief, or as the bible calls it, faith; or it will be the belief that what I've proclaimed is a lie. This second alternative, unfortunately, only mirrors the lie you're living by. It also demonstrates a lack in your ability to rightly discern truth when it is presented to you. But remember God does not intend for any to perish. So be ready when this message happens to you again, because it is God's way of making sure you get past being you.

"I want to thank Pastor Tim and his lovely wife for having me here these past couple of days." Looking towards the back of the room, Leon continued, "Young William, I want to thank you for being available for us to learn so much from you." Turning toward the side of the auditorium and giving a wave of his hand, he responded, "Bill, I want to thank you for your input and strength in this house. I trust you've been challenged by what I've said and are now prepared to deliver the best you've ever given. The days ahead will pale in comparison to the history you've experienced. The Father is not done with you yet." Bill raised his cane in acknowledgement to Leon's gratitude.

"Let me close with a prayer for you," Leon said as he raised his arms up towards the ceiling. "Father, in the days and weeks ahead I ask that you will bring to these people here tonight a deep abiding revelation of your immense love for them. Show them just how worthy they are to you and the overwhelming price your love paid for them to be brought into the family. Let them now walk into the fullness of the grace you gave to them on the day they became a new creation. Open the eyes of their understanding so they may be able to see just how perfectly you see them right now. Father, I thank you for loving us and never leaving us. May the days ahead be a manifestation of the glory you have placed within each of us. In the name of your Son we say that it is to be so. Amen."

"Amen," loudly rumbled throughout the crowd as heads rose to see Leon gather his materials and walk towards the door. Tim quickly rose from his seat and announced, "Thanks everyone. We'll see you on Sunday morning." Several people quickly gathered around Tim asking him questions as he watched Leon disappear out the door into the hallway.

Chapter 14

As the last notes of the music were dissipating throughout the auditorium, Tim approached the up-ended lectern from last week's service. "Thank you everyone. That was glorious once again," he said watching the worship team descend the stairs of the platform. Pausing for a moment to allow everyone to take their seat, Tim scanned the congregation.

"It is good to see all of you that returned this week. How many of you are new to our services here today?" Tim asked looking out over the crowd for any raised hands. After seeking for a long moment with no apparent results, Tim continued.

"As you can see there have been a few changes since last week's message," he said pointing to the lectern on the floor. "Is there anybody here today that wasn't here last week?" As Tim peered out to the crowd a few hands scattered around the auditorium rose. "Keep your hands up and wave to me to let me know that you've since talked to someone here who explained all that transpired."

Tim watched as all the hands waved back to him. "Good. I won't need to explain everything that went on then. It's possible that you may have heard that there have been a few other changes which have been going on as a result of last week meetings. I want to confirm that yes, as Bob Dylan said, the times they are a changing.

"Before I get too far into that, I want to affirm all that Leon stated here in the meetings we held last weekend. I fully stand behind every claim that he made. For those of you that might believe that I just brought him in here on the spur the moment, rest assured that I spent several months talking with Leon about this body before I even set a date for him to speak. It was only after that time of counsel did I invited him here to shake us up and put us back on track for what the Lord has intended for us.

"I have spent the past few days seeking God about just what my role is to be in this endeavor and how I'm to facilitate the work He has in mind. I'm still leaning into Him for answers but I feel that He has shown me some things which I'll roll out in the days ahead.

"For today though I want to spring off of where Leon took us last week. As you may recall he spoke about the new covenant as described in 31st chapter of the book of Jeremiah. One of the main characteristics that that passages describes is where every one would know the Lord and there would be no need for teaching.

"We have taught a lot of things about the Lord here and yet it was never in alignment with what He clearly defined in this vital passage of the new covenant. Some of it may have been 'new covenant' concepts but they were always shrouded in the Law. We can't have a mixture of the two. It is going to be one or the other. For my part, I'm purposely going to stay away from the teaching that I've followed from the past that were based from the law.

"I hereby intend to apply myself to teaching only those things that flow from God's grace. Having said this, I also know that teaching is no longer a sacred position in this new covenant. So what am I going to teach on? Well, let me start here. Go with me to the book of Titus and I'm going to read you a couple of verses and then try to explain this direction we're headed in," Tim said raising his bible up which he had been carrying.

"Go with me to the 2nd chapter of Titus and find verse 11 and 12. They read,

> *(11) For the grace of God that brings salvation hath appeared to all men, (12) Teaching us that, denying ungodliness and worldly lusts, we should live soberly, righteously, and godly, in this present world;*

"Verse 11 states that the grace of God has appeared to all men bringing salvation. Now we know salvation only came through Jesus. So according to this verse, Jesus and the grace of God is one in the same. But look at the next verse which is a continuation of verse 11. It says that grace, or Jesus, will teach us to live soberly, righteously, and godly lives.

"Now I want to bring this point out to you. 1 John 4:17 states that as Jesus is so, are we in this world. Much of what we call teaching about the 'Jesus-kind-of-life' deals with the Jesus who fulfilled the Law. However, both Paul and John are referring to the Jesus that instigated a new covenant. As He, Jesus, is in the new covenant, so are we in this world, today and then tomorrow. This is who, this is the grace which will teach us to live soberly, righteous, and godly lives.

"I cannot teach you this. There isn't one person here that can do it either. The reason why is simple: the moment we try to, it will be the Law. It will use statements like, 'You must; you need to; you can't;' so on and so on. We'll be forced to make blanket statements that try to cover all the bases in all of your lives knowing full well that you are all unique and there is no way we can possibly know every possible condition in your lives that you face. So even though our teaching will have the appearance of good, godly counsel, honestly, it is just a crap shoot.

"So what are you, what are we to do? How many of you think Jesus knows how to live a godly life today?" Tim earnestly asked the congregation. Hands quickly rose in response. "Hold on a minute. That might seem too easy a question to answer. Let me put some perspective on it. The godly life under the Law meant that you were able to complete the rules that would bring the favor of God into your life for all to see just how blessed you were. We do not fall under those parameters any longer if we're new covenant believers.

"What then does it mean to live a godly life to a new covenant believer? Simply it means living in the reality that God resides in us. This is a new creation, a new covenant reality that only Jesus can teach us. In the old covenant, God only came upon a person to enable them to perform a task and then left. We on the other hand, always abide with Him. He is always with us even in all of our stuff. Wherever we are, so is God. 24/7. No holidays. Do you understand?

"Under the Law there was always the question of whether God would hear your prayer or see your sacrifice. Not with us.

Consider that when you raid the refrigerator late at night, he knows what sandwich is best for you. Or when you go into the shower, he's there counting the minutes that you're using up the hot water for the next person, trying to nudge you to get out faster. When you screw up at work, at home, with your wife, husband, kids, parents, neighbor, yes, even with me, he is there. When you pick your nose or scratch your... you get the point, he is there. This can freak out a lot of people. That is why we need Jesus to teach how to live a life where God is everywhere and in everything we do.

"Leon came here and pointed out the nature of sin consciousness that ruled our daily lives. It focused more on our thought about us rather than the thoughts of God. Now we need to take heed to his advice and start to live a new covenant life according to the truth found in the scriptures. I openly admit this will not be easy for most of you, myself included. But I am determined to not preach any three, four, five, or six point sermons again. I owe it to you to see that we move together into the new nature as a body. Some of you may be there already. All I ask is that you give the rest of us the opportunity to catch up with you.

"Let me make something clear about this process. If any of you feel that this is not a direction that you can travel, the doors are always open for you to go through them and my blessing will go with you." Tim paused for several minutes to allow the weight of his remark to have its fullest impact.

"I want to have you understand that I'm as skittish about this new direction as the rest of you may be. However, I know without question, that if we were to continue in the direction that we were headed, I would not be here in three months leading you anywhere. I am extremely excited about what lies ahead for us since it will be truly directed by Holy Spirit. I know that in the days, weeks and months ahead we will be growing in our awareness of our individual relationship with the trinity. It will be from this new found intimacy that we will then move corporately in this community.

"There are a number of programs that we presently support and operate through this church. They will still continue to aid those people who have come to rely on them. We will however look at each and every one of them to see that they are functioning from the new understanding of our relationship with the Father. This means that those of you who have leadership and assisting roles will be under greater scrutiny to demonstrate how this new direction in relating to the Father will come to your roles. I know that some of you will have no problem with this while some of you it may take a few tries to get in the flow of things.

"I'm saying these things corporately for the sole purpose of making sure that everyone is on the same page. I know that many of you don't really know all that goes on behind the scenes in this ministry, which is truly my fault. But I believe that we need to let all of you be sensitive to the many roles we perform here in our community. I trust that as you become more aware, we, as a body, will be better able to imitate our heavenly relationship to those we serve and see a greater move of the Lord in the lives of these people.

"Lastly, for those of you who feel that I'm throwing out the baby with the bath water, rest assured that this is not the case. The core beliefs and mission of this church is still the same. I am simply casting a new light upon them which aligns more to the new covenant realities we should have been operating from all along. I take full responsibility for how we got here just as I'll take full responsibility for where were headed. The advantage that I have this time around is that the Father will be leading us and my responsibility will be simply to hear and enter into what He has already accomplished.

"So with that being said, if you could all stand while I close us out in prayer," Tim said lifting his hands to signal for the congregation to rise. "I know that this has not been a barn burner of a message today and it has been somewhat shorter than normal. I feel that I've expressed my heart for this body. You don't need hype or long-windedness to do that. So if you would bow your heads with me, Father, we offer our thanks to you in how you care so much for each and every one of us. We stand amazed at the generosity that you have poured out upon us and how you have taken everything into consideration so that we could come into the royal fellowship of your family. You truly deserve our highest regard and adoration.

"Jesus, we thank you for standing in our place at the cross. Our gratitude cannot be adequately expressed for the great gifts that you have poured out to each one of us. We deeply appreciate that you intercede daily on our behalf to the Father. We are grateful for the divine healing that you have secured for our bodies, and that as you are in the world, so are we.

"Holy Spirit, we greet your presence in our lives with open arms. Thank you for revealing Jesus to us and drawing us into a deeper relationship with Him. We ask, as Paul has, that we would have a greater revelation of the height and length and depth and breadth of the Father's love for us. Thank you for teaching us and guiding us into our new nature. We offer ourselves as willing vessels to be used to extend the kingdom of God on this earth. And all those who believe say, Amen." A loud "amen" rolled throughout the congregation.

"Thank you everyone and we'll see you next week. Come expecting more changes. Love you," Tim responded as people began to leave the auditorium. "That went pretty good," he said under his breath as he approached the center aisle while several people began coming to him with questions. "Okay, one at a time. We're just getting started here so give me a little breathing room," Tim said as he reached out and shook the hand of the first person in line.

Chapter 15

Tim rushed through the door of his office to answer the phone which had been incessantly ringing. "Hello. Pastor Tim. How may I help you?"

"How you holding up, Tim."

"Leon?" Tim asked with excitement. "Man it's good to hear from you. We seem to be holding our own around here. How have you been?"

"Doing well my friend. Look, I wanted to check in with you and see how you're handling things. I know I kinda left you in a hurry, but I had a commitment with another pastor I had to attend to…"

"No, that's fine. I know you're busy. I really appreciate you checking in. You know you were spot on when you said that there would be some fallout from what you preached on. The day after you left, I had one of my associate pastors tell me that if what you proclaimed to the body about not taking anything which looks like the law from the leadership, then he would have to leave."

"Really! What did you do?" Leon inquired eagerly.

"Held the door open for him as he left in a state of bewilderment," Tim laughed.

"Way to go!" Leon laughed heartily along with Tim. "How your people handling things?"

"It seems like I've been running non-stop since you left. Not in a bad sense. These people are pulling me into their group bible studies, men's group meeting, breakfast clubs…you name it. I've not seen such hunger in them…ever! I did begin a Monday night service as an introduction into the grace message. We had over 100 people on the first night! It seems that most of them are people who never attended regular services because they work on Sundays."

"Fantastic. How has…um…what's his name…Bill, yeah Bill, how's he been doing in all of this?" Leon inquired eagerly.

"Well, within the first couple of weeks he was rather withdrawn around here. I didn't know what may have been going on with him since it almost looked like he was intentionally avoiding me."

"Really?" Leon responded quietly. "Was he saying anything to anyone?"

"No. That's what was strange. The people who looked up to him for guidance the most and often told me previously what Bill had said, weren't even mentioning him to me. It was like some kind of contagious disease had hit him and no one wanted a part of him."

"That's not good!"

"Yeah, I know. So I invited him to coffee one morning and we had a really good talk about everything. He told me how he understood why I brought you in. He felt that much of what you said about the way teaching was being presented to the body was really directed towards him since he had been here so long."

"Well, not him alone," Leon interjected.

"I let him know that too. Bill just felt it would be best for everyone for him to step back and allow the events to take their natural course. I told him I fully understand his approach but I wasn't comfortable with it in this matter. I asked him to be my point man in the body. I told him I wanted him to bring anything he hears, whatever it is directly to me so the two of us can address it properly. If there were questions about the teachings, I wanted him to feel free to bring clarity to those who came to him. Foremost, I wanted him to know I value his service over all these years and to not think he was done yet."

"Good for you, Tim!" Leon happily exclaimed.

"Thanks. I introduced Bill's new role to the congregation and he seems more active than I've seen him in a long time."

There was a moment of silence before Leon spoke. "So let me ask the big question. How is Lisa?"

"Yeah, that is the big question. I know she is better able to answer this than me, but…you know Leon, she really got hit hard and it's taking a while for her to come back to this lifestyle again.

She pretty much said, 'screw all of you' when she left this office. I was pretty much in the same condition too. So now, seeing all the work I'm doing and…and the joy I'm receiving in the process of it, I can sense she is beginning to see the difference can be beneficial if she wants to take it up again.

"I'll say this though; there are a number of ladies who in the past did not really have much interest in being around her. I have noticed how Lisa has really taken an interest in them and is kinda pursuing them…if I can call it that. She tries to go out to coffee with a couple of them each week and do the mall thing with them. I know she wouldn't do this before but now it seems to have helped her a bit."

"That sounds encouraging, Tim. So you still want to give this up?" Leon quipped.

"Every day," Tim laughed. "Then I get out of bed and can't wait to see what the Father has planned for me the day. You know Leon, I've almost thrown out my day planner. I've come to such a point of relying on Him to show me what to do that I don't really know the last time I checked my calendar to schedule an appointment. It's weird! I use to be so attached to it, but now I can't live with it. And speaking of schedules, when you going to be around these parts again? The pulpit is always laying down for you here," Tim snickered.

"Yeah?" Leon chuckled. "I'm not too certain, since my calendar is like yours. I'll have to see what the Father's leadings are over the next few months. I appreciate the offer and I'm certain we can come together soon.

"Look, I've got to go, but before I do I want to encourage you to keep true to the message. Some will not appreciate how you deliver it but they'll move on. Your purpose is simply to keep your people growing in maturity without getting them attached to you through rules and regulations. You'll know when you get there when the people don't ask you for advice but rather give insight. Love you, Tim, and send Lisa my best. Talk to you soon. Bye."

"Thanks, Leon," and then the dial tone blared in Tim's ear. "Love you too…" Tim softly said as he hung up the phone. Suddenly, a gentle knock came on his door. "Pastor Tim, are you available?" came a quivering voice. "More and more every day," Tim joyfully exclaimed as he reached for the door. "Come on in."

Scripture Reference

While this is a fictional story, the core of its message does come from actual scriptures found in the bible. While several of the passages were included in the story, there were also a number of references which were made within the text without actually citing where they were in the bible. In order to accommodate any questions you might have had with these passages, I've included in this section the actual verses as a study guide to assist you.

Chapter 2

Romans 8:1
(1) There is therefore now no condemnation to them which are in Christ Jesus, who walk not after the flesh, but after the Spirit.

Jeremiah 31:31-34
(31) Behold, the days come, saith the LORD, that I will make a new covenant with the house of Israel, and with the house of Judah:
(32) Not according to the covenant that I made with their fathers in the day that I took them by the hand to bring them out of the land of Egypt; which my covenant they brake, although I was an husband unto them, saith the LORD:
(33) But this shall be the covenant that I will make with the house of Israel; After those days, saith the LORD, I will put my law in their inward parts, and write it in their hearts; and will be their God, and they shall be my people.
(34) And they shall teach no more every man his neighbour, and every man his brother, saying, Know the LORD: for they shall all know me, from the least of them unto the greatest of them, saith the LORD: for I will forgive their iniquity, and I will remember their sin no more.

Matthew 18:2-6
(2) And Jesus called a little child unto him, and set him in the midst of them,
(3) And said, Verily I say unto you, Except ye be converted, and become as little children, ye shall not enter into the kingdom of heaven.
(4) Whosoever therefore shall humble himself as this little child, the same is greatest in the kingdom of heaven.
(5) And whoso shall receive one such little child in my name receiveth me.
(6) But whoso shall offend one of these little ones which believe in me, it were better for him that a millstone were hanged about his neck, and that he were drowned in the depth of the sea.

Chapter 3

1 Timothy 3:6
(6) Not a novice, lest being lifted up with pride he fall into the condemnation of the devil.

Chapter 4

1 John 3:8
(8) He that committeth sin is of the devil; for the devil sinneth from the beginning. For this purpose the Son of God was manifested, that he might destroy the works of the devil.

Genesis 2:17
(17) But of the tree of the knowledge of good and evil, thou shalt not eat of it: for in the day that thou eatest thereof thou shalt surely die.

Matthew 18:14
(14) Even so it is not the will of your Father which is in heaven, that one of these little ones should perish.

Hebrews 4:9-11
(9) There remaineth therefore a rest to the people of God.
(10) For he that is entered into his rest, he also hath ceased from his own works, as God did from his.

(11) Let us labour therefore to enter into that rest, lest any man fall after the same example of unbelief.

Chapter 5

Revelation 21:1-3
(1) And I saw a new heaven and a new earth: for the first heaven and the first earth were passed away; and there was no more sea.
(2) And I John saw the holy city, new Jerusalem, coming down from God out of heaven, prepared as a bride adorned for her husband.
(3) And I heard a great voice out of heaven saying, Behold, the tabernacle of God is with men, and he will dwell with them, and they shall be his people, and God himself shall be with them, and be their God.

1 John 4:18
(18) There is no fear in love; but perfect love casteth out fear: because fear hath torment. He that feareth is not made perfect in love.

Chapter 6

Galatians 1:6-8
(6) I marvel that ye are so soon removed from him that called you into the grace of Christ unto another gospel:
(7) Which is not another; but there be some that trouble you, and would pervert the gospel of Christ.
(8) But though we, or an angel from heaven, preach any other gospel unto you than that which we have preached unto you, let him be accursed.

Chapter 7

Ephesians 2:11-16
(11) Wherefore remember, that ye being in time past Gentiles in the flesh, who are called Uncircumcision by that which is called the Circumcision in the flesh made by hands;

(12) That at that time ye were without Christ, being aliens from the commonwealth of Israel, and strangers from the covenants of promise, having no hope, and without God in the world:
(13) But now in Christ Jesus ye who sometimes were far off are made nigh by the blood of Christ.
(14) For he is our peace, who hath made both one, and hath broken down the middle wall of partition between us;
(15) Having abolished in his flesh the enmity, even the law of commandments contained in ordinances; for to make in himself of twain one new man, so making peace;
(16) And that he might reconcile both unto God in one body by the cross, having slain the enmity thereby:

Galatians 4:4
(4) But when the fulness of the time was come, God sent forth his Son, made of a woman, made under the law,

Hebrews 10:3-4
(3) But in those sacrifices there is a remembrance again made of sins every year.
(4) For it is not possible that the blood of bulls and of goats should take away sins.

John 10:10
(10) The thief cometh not, but for to steal, and to kill, and to destroy: I am come that they might have life, and that they might have it more abundantly.

Judges 7:4-7
(4) And the LORD said unto Gideon, The people are yet too many; bring them down unto the water, and I will try them for thee there: and it shall be, that of whom I say unto thee, This shall go with thee, the same shall go with thee; and of whomsoever I say unto thee, This shall not go with thee, the same shall not go.
(5) So he brought down the people unto the water: and the LORD said unto Gideon, Every one that lappeth of the water with his tongue, as a dog lappeth, him shalt thou set by himself; likewise every one that boweth down upon his knees to drink.

(6) And the number of them that lapped, putting their hand to their mouth, were three hundred men: but all the rest of the people bowed down upon their knees to drink water.
(7) And the LORD said unto Gideon, By the three hundred men that lapped will I save you, and deliver the Midianites into thine hand: and let all the other people go every man unto his place.

Isaiah 55:8-9
(8) For my thoughts are not your thoughts, neither are your ways my ways, saith the LORD.
(9) For as the heavens are higher than the earth, so are my ways higher than your ways, and my thoughts than your thoughts.

John 3:16
(16) For God so loved the world, that he gave his only begotten Son, that whosoever believeth in him should not perish, but have everlasting life.

Jeremiah 31:31-34
(31) Behold, the days come, saith the LORD, that I will make a new covenant with the house of Israel, and with the house of Judah:
(32) Not according to the covenant that I made with their fathers in the day that I took them by the hand to bring them out of the land of Egypt; which my covenant they brake, although I was an husband unto them, saith the LORD:
(33) But this shall be the covenant that I will make with the house of Israel; After those days, saith the LORD, I will put my law in their inward parts, and write it in their hearts; and will be their God, and they shall be my people.
(34) And they shall teach no more every man his neighbour, and every man his brother, saying, Know the LORD: for they shall all know me, from the least of them unto the greatest of them, saith the LORD: for I will forgive their iniquity, and I will remember their sin no more.

Galatians 3:13-18
(13) Christ hath redeemed us from the curse of the law, being made a curse for us: for it is written, Cursed is every one that hangeth on a tree:

(14) That the blessing of Abraham might come on the Gentiles through Jesus Christ; that we might receive the promise of the Spirit through faith.

(15) Brethren, I speak after the manner of men; Though it be but a man's covenant, yet if it be confirmed, no man disannulleth, or addeth thereto.

(16) Now to Abraham and his seed were the promises made. He saith not, And to seeds, as of many; but as of one, And to thy seed, which is Christ.

(17) And this I say, that the covenant, that was confirmed before of God in Christ, the law, which was four hundred and thirty years after, cannot disannul, that it should make the promise of none effect.

(18) For if the inheritance be of the law, it is no more of promise: but God gave it to Abraham by promise.

Genesis 17:1-8

(1) And when Abram was ninety years old and nine, the LORD appeared to Abram, and said unto him, I am the Almighty God; walk before me, and be thou perfect.

(2) And I will make my covenant between me and thee, and will multiply thee exceedingly.

(3) And Abram fell on his face: and God talked with him, saying,

(4) As for me, behold, my covenant is with thee, and thou shalt be a father of many nations.

(5) Neither shall thy name any more be called Abram, but thy name shall be Abraham; for a father of many nations have I made thee.

(6) And I will make thee exceeding fruitful, and I will make nations of thee, and kings shall come out of thee.

(7) And I will establish my covenant between me and thee and thy seed after thee in their generations for an everlasting covenant, to be a God unto thee, and to thy seed after thee.

(8) And I will give unto thee, and to thy seed after thee, the land wherein thou art a stranger, all the land of Canaan, for an everlasting possession; and I will be their God.

Genesis 15:3-6

(3) And Abram said, Behold, to me thou hast given no seed: and, lo, one born in my house is mine heir.

(4) And, behold, the word of the LORD came unto him, saying, This shall not be thine heir; but he that shall come forth out of thine own bowels shall be thine heir.
(5) And he brought him forth abroad, and said, Look now toward heaven, and tell the stars, if thou be able to number them: and he said unto him, So shall thy seed be.
(6) And he believed in the LORD; and he counted it to him for righteousness.

Chapter 8

Exodus 3:4-6
(4) And when the LORD saw that he turned aside to see, God called unto him out of the midst of the bush, and said, Moses, Moses. And he said, Here am I.
(5) And he said, Draw not nigh hither: put off thy shoes from off thy feet, for the place whereon thou standest is holy ground.
(6) Moreover he said, I am the God of thy father, the God of Abraham, the God of Isaac, and the God of Jacob. And Moses hid his face; for he was afraid to look upon God.

Genesis 15:12-14
(12) And when the sun was going down, a deep sleep fell upon Abram; and, lo, an horror of great darkness fell upon him.
(13) And he said unto Abram, Know of a surety that thy seed shall be a stranger in a land that is not theirs, and shall serve them; and they shall afflict them four hundred years;
(14) And also that nation, whom they shall serve, will I judge: and afterward shall they come out with great substance.

Exodus 19:4-8
(4) Ye have seen what I did unto the Egyptians, and how I bare you on eagles' wings, and brought you unto myself.
(5) Now therefore, if ye will obey my voice indeed, and keep my covenant, then ye shall be a peculiar treasure unto me above all people: for all the earth is mine:
(6) And ye shall be unto me a kingdom of priests, and an holy nation. These are the words which thou shalt speak unto the children of Israel.

(7) And Moses came and called for the elders of the people, and laid before their faces all these words which the LORD commanded him.
(8) And all the people answered together, and said, All that the LORD hath spoken we will do. And Moses returned the words of the people unto the LORD.

Galatians 3:19
(19) Wherefore then serveth the law? It was added because of transgressions, till the seed should come to whom the promise was made; and it was ordained by angels in the hand of a mediator.

Romans 4:15
(15) Because the law worketh wrath: for where no law is, there is no transgression.

Romans 5:13
(13) (For until the law sin was in the world: but sin is not imputed when there is no law.

Romans 5:20
(20) Moreover the law entered, that the offence might abound. But where sin abounded, grace did much more abound:

Mark 7:13
(13) Making the word of God of none effect through your tradition, which ye have delivered: and many such like things do ye.

John 5:17-20
(17) But Jesus answered them, My Father worketh hitherto, and I work.
(18) Therefore the Jews sought the more to kill him, because he not only had broken the sabbath, but said also that God was his Father, making himself equal with God.
(19) Then answered Jesus and said unto them, Verily, verily, I say unto you, The Son can do nothing of himself, but what he seeth the Father do: for what things soever he doeth, these also doeth the Son likewise.
(20) For the Father loveth the Son, and sheweth him all things that himself doeth: and he will shew him greater works than these, that ye may marvel.

John 14:6-7
(6) Jesus saith unto him, I am the way, the truth, and the life: no man cometh unto the Father, but by me.
(7) If ye had known me, ye should have known my Father also: and from henceforth ye know him, and have seen him.

Chapter 10

1 John 3:4-9
(4) Whosoever committeth sin transgresseth also the law: for sin is the transgression of the law.
(5) And ye know that he was manifested to take away our sins; and in him is no sin.
(6) Whosoever abideth in him sinneth not: whosoever sinneth hath not seen him, neither known him.
(7) Little children, let no man deceive you: he that doeth righteousness is righteous, even as he is righteous.
(8) He that committeth sin is of the devil; for the devil sinneth from the beginning. For this purpose the Son of God was manifested, that he might destroy the works of the devil.
(9) Whosoever is born of God doth not commit sin; for his seed remaineth in him: and he cannot sin, because he is born of God.

Hebrews 10:1-4
(1) For the law having a shadow of good things to come, and not the very image of the things, can never with those sacrifices which they offered year by year continually make the comers thereunto perfect.
(2) For then would they not have ceased to be offered? because that the worshippers once purged should have had no more conscience of sins.
(3) But in those sacrifices there is a remembrance again made of sins every year.
(4) For it is not possible that the blood of bulls and of goats should take away sins.

Hebrews 10:9-10

(9) Then said he, Lo, I come to do thy will, O God. He taketh away the first, that he may establish the second.

(10) By the which will we are sanctified through the offering of the body of Jesus Christ once for all.

Hebrews 10:14

(14) For by one offering he hath perfected for ever them that are sanctified.

Luke 22:19-20

(19) And he took bread, and gave thanks, and brake it, and gave unto them, saying, This is my body which is given for you: this do in remembrance of me.

(20) Likewise also the cup after supper, saying, This cup is the new testament in my blood, which is shed for you.

Hebrews 10:24-27

(24) And let us consider one another to provoke unto love and to good works:

(25) Not forsaking the assembling of ourselves together, as the manner of some is; but exhorting one another: and so much the more, as ye see the day approaching.

(26) For if we sin wilfully after that we have received the knowledge of the truth, there remaineth no more sacrifice for sins,

(27) But a certain fearful looking for of judgment and fiery indignation, which shall devour the adversaries.

James 1:5-8

(5) If any of you lack wisdom, let him ask of God, that giveth to all men liberally, and upbraideth not; and it shall be given him.

(6) But let him ask in faith, nothing wavering. For he that wavereth is like a wave of the sea driven with the wind and tossed.

(7) For let not that man think that he shall receive any thing of the Lord.

(8) A double minded man is unstable in all his ways.

Chapter 11

Revelation 12:7-10
(7) And there was war in heaven: Michael and his angels fought against the dragon; and the dragon fought and his angels,
(8) And prevailed not; neither was their place found any more in heaven.
(9) And the great dragon was cast out, that old serpent, called the Devil, and Satan, which deceiveth the whole world: he was cast out into the earth, and his angels were cast out with him.
(10) And I heard a loud voice saying in heaven, Now is come salvation, and strength, and the kingdom of our God, and the power of his Christ: for the accuser of our brethren is cast down, which accused them before our God day and night.

Hebrews 10:18
(18) Now where remission of these is, there is no more offering for sin.

Romans 10:4
(4) For Christ is the end of the law for righteousness to every one that believeth.

Chapter 13

Luke 2:42-50
(42) And when he was twelve years old, they went up to Jerusalem after the custom of the feast.
(43) And when they had fulfilled the days, as they returned, the child Jesus tarried behind in Jerusalem; and Joseph and his mother knew not of it.
(44) But they, supposing him to have been in the company, went a day's journey; and they sought him among their kinsfolk and acquaintance.
(45) And when they found him not, they turned back again to Jerusalem, seeking him.
(46) And it came to pass, that after three days they found him in the temple, sitting in the midst of the doctors, both hearing them, and asking them questions.

(47) And all that heard him were astonished at his understanding and answers.
(48) And when they saw him, they were amazed: and his mother said unto him, Son, why hast thou thus dealt with us? behold, thy father and I have sought thee sorrowing.
(49) And he said unto them, How is it that ye sought me? wist ye not that I must be about my Father's business?
(50) And they understood not the saying which he spake unto them.

Proverbs 20:9
(9) Who can say, I have made my heart clean, I am pure from my sin?

Proverbs 4:23
(23) Keep thy heart with all diligence; for out of it are the issues of life.

1 Samuel 16:7
(7) But the LORD said unto Samuel, Look not on his countenance, or on the height of his stature; because I have refused him: for the LORD seeth not as man seeth; for man looketh on the outward appearance, but the LORD looketh on the heart.

Luke 6:45
(45) A good man out of the good treasure of his heart bringeth forth that which is good; and an evil man out of the evil treasure of his heart bringeth forth that which is evil: for of the abundance of the heart his mouth speaketh.

1 Corinthians 3:16
(16) Know ye not that ye are the temple of God, and that the Spirit of God dwelleth in you?

Romans 12:2
(2) And be not conformed to this world: but be ye transformed by the renewing of your mind, that ye may prove what is that good, and acceptable, and perfect, will of God.

Ezekiel 36:25-27
(25) Then will I sprinkle clean water upon you, and ye shall be clean: from all your filthiness, and from all your idols, will I cleanse you.
(26) A new heart also will I give you, and a new spirit will I put within you: and I will take away the stony heart out of your flesh, and I will give you an heart of flesh.
(27) And I will put my spirit within you, and cause you to walk in my statutes, and ye shall keep my judgments, and do them.

Colossians 2:11
(11) In whom also ye are circumcised with the circumcision made without hands, in putting off the body of the sins of the flesh by the circumcision of Christ:

Deuteronomy 30:6
(6) And the LORD thy God will circumcise thine heart, and the heart of thy seed, to love the LORD thy God with all thine heart, and with all thy soul, that thou mayest live.

2 Corinthians 5:17
(17) Therefore if any man be in Christ, he is a new creature: old things are passed away; behold, all things are become new.

James 2:8
(8) If ye fulfil the royal law according to the scripture, Thou shalt love thy neighbour as thyself, ye do well:

1 John 4:7-8
(7) Beloved, let us love one another: for love is of God; and every one that loveth is born of God, and knoweth God.
(8) He that loveth not knoweth not God; for God is love.

John 10:10
(10) The thief cometh not, but for to steal, and to kill, and to destroy: I am come that they might have life, and that they might have it more abundantly.

Hebrews 11:6
(6) But without faith it is impossible to please him: for he that cometh to God must believe that he is, and that he is a rewarder of them that diligently seek him.

Ephesians 2:6
(6) And hath raised us up together, and made us sit together in heavenly places in Christ Jesus:

John 16:7-9
(7) Nevertheless I tell you the truth; It is expedient for you that I go away: for if I go not away, the Comforter will not come unto you; but if I depart, I will send him unto you.
(8) And when he is come, he will reprove the world of sin, and of righteousness, and of judgment:
(9) Of sin, because they believe not on me;

Chapter 14

Titus 2:11-12
(11) For the grace of God that bringeth salvation hath appeared to all men,
(12) Teaching us that, denying ungodliness and worldly lusts, we should live soberly, righteously, and godly, in this present world;

About the Author

Mike and his family live in Portland, Oregon, where he is one of the teachers of the Word of God at a local fellowship. As a graduate of the Latin University of Theology, Mike is passionate about people understanding what grace looks like in the Kingdom of God, its impact in their lives and how it changes communities who are determined to operate from its authority.

Mike is the author of *Grace for Shame, Chesed: Beyond the Veil of Mercy, Your Life is a Freaking Mess and You Want Answers, A Kingdom Primer, Eternal Life. Yes Forever!* and *My Grace to You.* Mike contributes his insights about the Kingdom of grace at www.mygrace2u.com and www.graceforshame.com.

Mike can be contacted at mike@mikehillebrecht.com

Additional titles by mike hillebrecht

What if what you knew from scriptures about mercy wasn't quite accurate? What if the blessings that we've been searching for have been locked away all this time in a simple Hebrew word that scholars agree has no English translation?

In this brief expose, teacher and author Mike Hillebrecht (Grace for Shame) explores the meaning of a Hebrew term that the original Bible scholars may have interpreted inaccurately into the Greek word we know as 'mercy." You will begin to see how many of the Old and New Testament passages take on an entirely different meaning by understanding this key Hebrew word in its proper context.

Mike will take you through a practical explanation of the full meaning of coming to the throne of grace in God's Kingdom not with the expectation of judgment but with the fullest measure of equality. This is an eye-opening study that will impact your walk with the Lord and those that are around you.

Chesed – Beyond the Veil of Mercy
ISBN/EAN13: 0615617352 / 9780615617350
Page Count: 70
Trim Size: 6"x 9"
Language: English
Color: Black and White
Related Categories: Religion / Biblical Studies / General

www.beyondthemercyveil.com

Shame. Embarrassment. Humiliation. The ugly trio. Their distinct occupation is to keep you seeing yourself as a sinner saved by grace rather than as a son seated next to the throne of grace. The distinction is about whether you are being reigned over or whether you're reigning. It's a battle for your predestined role in the Kingdom of God.

Inside *Grace for Shame* you will discover a fresh look at what grace truly looks like and how God designed it to operate in your life. This ain't your papa or mama's grace - this is grace straight from the Kingdom of God as it has been operating throughout all of eternity. You will find the grace that is intended to break off the shackles that the ugly trio has bound you with, imprisoning you from your destiny.

Expect to finally identify with the true kingdom meaning of the cross - not the sanitized message that religion has produced. Are you considered a prodigal son, or know someone who is? *Grace for Shame* gives a perspective from the Kingdom of God that it's not about your past but about how truly great you are right now in the eyes of the Father.

Grace for Shame
ISBN/EAN13: 0615605508 / 9780615605500
Page Count: 220
Trim Size: 6"x 9"
Language: English
Color: Black and White
Related Categories: Religion / Christian Life / Personal Growth

www.graceforshame.com

Most people study grace from the position of the fall of man. This makes grace an escape mechanism to get you into Heaven. But what if that wasn't the original intent of grace for you?

In *My Grace to You*, author mike hillebrecht takes a fresh look at grace from the Kingdom of God viewpoint before the foundation of the world. In this insightful reading you will discover why understanding how the New Testament writers use of grace in their daily social structures gave them an ability to activate the truths and power of the Kingdom of God quickly within their communities.

Drawing from a variety of sources, mike takes you on a well rounded tour of the meaning of grace that will open up possibilities which you may never knew existed. You can be certain that this isn't the grace your grandma knew – and it sure is a whole lot more exciting too!

My Grace to You
ISBN-13: 978-0615686622 (Custom)
ISBN-10: 0615686621
Trim Size: 6" x 9" (15.24 x 22.86 cm)
Color: Black & White on Cream paper
Page Count: 202 pages
Related Categories: Religion / Christian Life / Personal Growth

www.mygrace2u.com

If you desire to be known as a Son of God according to Romans 8, you had better know the 3-R's of the Kingdom. They are the foundational tenets of the kingdom's interaction with you as a son. The Holy Spirit will not advance you to the head of the class if you miss any one of the important lessons these have to demonstrate. Within this booklet you will find covered the following items:

The Father's intent – What was the original intent of God and how it changed.
Reconciliation – The Father's plan.
Redemption – The purpose of Jesus
Righteousness – The effect of reconciliation and redemption.
Right of Law – Where you are in God's time-line.
Royal Law – This is the one law given by the King.
Perfect Law – This is what we're striving to adhere too.
Peace – It may not be what you think.

As with the purpose of any primer, the entire spectrum of the topics offered cannot be presented to their fullest measure. This book is designed simply to be a building block which will provoke your thoughts about the matters at hand and spur you to search out further how they impact your walk with the Father.

A Kingdom Primer
ISBN/EAN13: 061562099X / 978-0615620992
Page Count: 126 pages
Trim Size: 6" x 9"
Language: English
Color: Black & White on White paper
Related Categories: Religion / Biblical Studies / General

www.kingdomprimer.com

Live and not die! This is not the motto of some whacked out group of mercenaries. It belongs to a select group of people who believe that what Jesus Christ accomplished at the cross is supposed to be the norm for their lives. What do you mean, "Thank goodness this isn't for me?"

Eternal life. Yes, Forever! is a stark look at a truth that has been turned sideways. Contained within, you will finally find the truth about the purpose of Heaven and how you're not supposed to go there except for dinner. Being "born again" versus being "saved" will be explored in relation to your dinner guests and football enthusiasts. You'll be re-introduced to the marvelous prefix "re" and see how this simple little construct, when it's added to a word, can screw up your entire theology.

Prepare to see death from an entirely different perspective as *Eternal Life. Yes, Forever!* takes off the gloves and slaps the enemy senseless once again.

Eternal Life. Yes, Forever!
ISBN-13: 978-0615623542 (Custom)
ISBN-10: 0615623549
Page Count: 140 pages
Trim Size: 6" x 9" (15.24 x 22.86 cm)
Color: Black & White on White paper
Related Categories Religion / Christian Life / Spiritual Growth

www.lifeyesforever.com

DID YOU LIKE THE BOOK?

It has been my hope that contained within the contents of this book there has been one item, possibly more, which has inspired you or brought clarity to the path you're now following. If this is the case, then I would like to hear from you about what you discovered. You can write me at mike@mikehillebrecht.com.

Within the spirit of grace contained within this message, there is one of several other things you can now do. Books are promoted mostly by word of mouth. So if you found this useful, tell a friend. Heck, tell all your friends. Mention it on Facebook or whatever other social medium you use. If you're so inclined, you could go onto Amazon.com, look up the book and press the like button. While you're there, write a short review, or a long one if you like, about what you felt the book meant to you. If you're really inspired, give a copy to a pastor. However, considering the message, caution might be advised on this last one.

If none of these things interest you, I understand. Many of us don't feel it is right to compel others to view matters such as grace on the same plane as us. After all there are better things to have a dialogue about and not risk the chance of turning people off. But isn't this the reason that the risk was originally taken by Jesus – to turn people. So what have you got to lose? It's not you, but Christ who lives in you.

Thank you and my sincere gratitude.

Mike

www.ingramcontent.com/pod-product-compliance
Lightning Source LLC
Chambersburg PA
CBHW071506040426
42444CB00008B/1514